A Man for Our Time

HILDE FIRTEL

*Foreword
by
Michael O'Carroll, C.S:Sp.*

THE MERCIER PRESS
CORK and DUBLIN

The Mercier Press Limited
4 Bridge Street, Cork
24 Lower Abbey Street, Dublin 1

© Hilde Firtel, 1985

Firtel, Hilde
A man for our time: Frank Duff and the Legion of Mary.
1. Duff, Frank. 2. Legion of Mary—Biography
3. Catholics—Ireland—Biography
I. Title
267'.182'0924   BX4705.D857

ISBN 0-85342-746-1

Printed by Litho Press Co. Ltd., Midleton, Co. Cork

Contents

Foreword	5
Preface	15
1. An Irish Family	16
2. Ascent – Interior and Exterior	19
3. A Very Special Apostolate	21
4. The Local Madman	25
5. Group Activity	27
6. The Spark that Caught	30
7. 7 September 1921	34
8. And Suddenly it Happened	37
9. The Incredible Venture	40
10. Assault on the Devil's Stronghold	44
11. A Movement takes Shape	49
12. The Burden is Growing	52
13. The Sign of the Cross	56
14. With Pope Pius XI	59
15. The First Envoys	61
16. By their Fruits	64
17. Far and Near	67
18. Into the Whole World	71
19. Big Crosses, Small Crosses, But always the Cross	76
20. Baptism of Fire in China	81
21. . . . And Rome has spoken once more	85
22. Sorrows and Joys	88
23. Alphonsus Lambe	91
24. . . . And yet the Miraculous was there	93

25.	New Flowers, New Sprouts	96
26.	Death Knocks at the Door	99
27.	Auditor at the Council	102
28.	'The Spirit of the Council'	107
29.	. . . And yet Life goes on	111
30.	Rome once more	113
31.	For Posterity	116
32.	The Last Days	118
33.	Mourning or Triumph?	121
34.	The Heritage	124
35.	Instead of an Epilogue	126

Foreword

I met Hilde Firtel on the occasion of her first visit to Dublin just after the war. I was introduced to her by Frank Duff who was at the same Legion function, a musical get-together. He was enthusiastic about this latest recruit to the band of heroic Legionary envoys. This brilliant girl – whom Frank commented could be taken for an Irish cailín – was going to spread the Legion in Germany. Interested readers will get the details in Hilde's story told by herself.

In this book she is paying what may perhaps be called a debt of honour. Like all of us who came in contact with this extraordinary man she was enriched. Her life was changed – changed utterly. I can think of few men in our time who had the gift to inspire, to lift the life of his listener to a different level, to open vistas hitherto undreamt of. I recall one meeting with him for lunch here in Blackrock College, where he had studied as a boy, when the conversation had turned on Mariology, that is the theology of Mary. I had read a good deal on the subject and have done so since then. Yet, as I wrote to him later that evening, I felt as if a band tightened around my head had snapped, and I was thinking in a free, unfettered way about Mary as I had never done before.

It was no doubt the impact of a man who had worked out in experience what the theologians were trying to tell us in recent times. The motivation of Frank Duff was utterly right. He was steeped in the writings of St Louis Marie Grignion de Montfort, the apostle of Mary's universal mediation, who, perhaps, if the wish of the present Holy Father is supported widely, will soon be proclaimed a Doctor of the Universal Church.

It is a thrilling story that Hilde Firtel tells. It was, even unconsciously, from the beginning under the sign of Mary. And as time passed, with the immense ferment of idealism and activity which was generated around the personality of Frank Duff, Mary's role was more fully and explicitly proclaimed.

It was the beginning of a Marian age in the Church, in the year 1921 when on 7 September the first meeting of the Legion took place. Another giant of the spirit, better known until then as a philosopher, educationist and national leader, Désiré Cardinal Mercier, had launched the movement on behalf of Mary's universal mediation of grace. Aided by theologians and patristic scholars of remarkable power and erudition, he had petitioned Rome for an Office and Mass of *Mary Mediatrix of all Graces*. He had published an enlightened pastoral letter on the subject with which he linked Blessed (as he still was) Louis Marie Grignion de Montfort's ideal of true devotion to Mary. He had then written to the bishops of the Catholic Church urging them to take advantage of the approval given by Rome and ask for the Office and Mass for their dioceses. He had hundreds of favourable replies.

Rome took account of the upsurge of Marian theology and Pius XI named three commissions, Roman, Spanish and Belgian, to study and report on the definability of Mary's universal mediation. The Pope did not publish a body of Marian doctrine. His successor, Pius XII more than made up the lack of such formal teaching. Elected on the eve of the Second World War he directed Catholic piety towards Mary as a most powerful advocate. In 1942 he consecrated the world to the Immaculate Heart of Mary – he was conscious of the fact that he had been consecrated bishop on 13 May 1917 on the moment that Our Lady was beginning her apparitions at Fatima. Some years after the war ended, in 1950, the Pope solemnly defined the dogma of the Assumption; four years later he proclaimed the universal Queenship of Mary. It came at the close of the Marian Year which he had declared for the centenary of the dogma of the Immaculate Conception – as he would dedicate another to the centenary in Lourdes the year he died.

Accompanying these events there were very many other notable movements and happenings, Marian and Mariological congresses, Marian societies, increasing pilgrimages to new and old shrines of Our Lady, a growing literature, theological, devotional, unequal as such production must be but evidence, none the less, of popular and, at times, sophisticated interest. Saints canonised in these years were sometimes of the kind to encourage Marian piety. Thus the saint of the Miraculous Medal, Catherine Labouré, was bound to affect all clients of Mary, especially members of the Legion of Mary. Still more so, the promotion, in the same year 1947, of St Louis Marie de Montfort to the ranks of the saints. Here was the inspiration of the Legion publicly acclaimed, exalted, approved by the Church – not that I would maintain that canonisation implies approval of every point of teaching, in the writings of the newly-declared saint. St Pius X had reference to the Legion, as had St Anthony Mary Claret.

That was the background in the Church to the lifework of Frank Duff. Coming to the more immediate environment in which he worked – the Irish situation in the early twenties, one is also seized by certain striking factors. In July 1921 a truce had been agreed between the British government and the Irish leaders of the War of Independence, which had gone on for over two years in the country. On 6 December a treaty was signed between plenipotentiaries of the Irish parliament, the Dáil, and representatives of the British government. We are not concerned here with the subsequent painful phase in Irish history. The significance for the Legion was that it was a first important foundation in the new Ireland – an Ireland enjoying a large measure of independence.

There is in fact a rich chapter to be written and studied in this very context. For when Frank Duff suddenly found himself faced with the problem of street girls ready to begin a new life but with nowhere to go, it was a minister of the then Free State government, Mr William T. Cosgrave, who provided the accommodation from government property. The dealings which Frank had with this man of strong Christian faith began one of the great friendships of his life. It was Mr Cosgrave, many years later, who suggested that Frank be given a papal honour. I am divulging a secret when I say that while Frank was in Rome for the Council in 1965, he had a clear preternatural sign of his friend's death at the moment it took place.

But we are ahead of events. This accolade, a nomination from the lay auditors to the Council, came late, as did other marks of ecclesiastical approval. Young people nowadays talk of their difficulties with the institutional Church. They would have little to tell the subject of Miss Firtel's book on the matter. He was not always understood, which is an under-statement, but he still went forward courageously, yet without rancour. No wonder he so relished the thought and the company of the angels.

In one area there was from an early date, and somewhat surprisingly, wholehearted encouragement. This was at the highest level of Church government. From the day on which Pius XI received him until the moment when he was invited to assist at Mass said by John Paul II in his private oratory and take breakfast with him afterwards, he enjoyed what, for a founder of a lay society, may well have been unique papal support. Not only in Rome where Pius XII received him, and from whence Paul VI and John XXIII sent him messages of the strongest approval and encouragement, but in the Nunciatures and Apostolic Delegations right round the world.

This was an organised chain of support. In the early critical days his staunchest backer in Dublin was Archbishop Paschal Robinson OFM, first Nuncio to an Irish government since the seventeenth century Italian Rinnucini, envoy to the Confederation of Kilkenny. Dr Robinson frequently invited Frank to his table in the Nunciature in Phoenix Park, when he would have with him distinguished ecclesiastics from abroad. It was an occasion to introduce the subject of the Legion, to explain it, to answer the kind of 'objections' then sometimes made, to exert that magic of his personality to which I have referred.

One legionary envoy after another has an eventful story to tell about the positive, generous means used by the Pope's representatives to help the extension of the Legion. It would be invidious to mention names, but none will object if I recall the immense prestige which Alfie Lambe (whose biographer Miss Firtel also has been) gained in the world of Latin America. The other case that springs to mind had worldwide repercussions through its sequel. Archbishop Riberi, a former secretary at the Dublin Nunciature, had seen and admired the work of Edel Quinn in East Africa where he was Delegate Apostolic. Named Pro-Nuncio to China some short time before the war achieved its devastating effects in the area, he proposed the Legion as an ideal instrument of evangelisation. In that, as many know he found a providential ally, Fr Aedan McGrath of the Columban Fathers. The heroic saga ended for many of the Chinese in the 'blood of martyrs' which we hope will be the seed of Christianity. For Fr McGrath it did not go to that limit, since he was not a native citizen of the state, but it meant long imprisonment from which, fortunately for many other countries in the Far East, he came out still resolute, convinced, indomitable.

The 'fall-out' of this operation was to prove quite unpredictable. A well-known Irish revolutionary and writer, Peadar O'Donnell, a Catholic, during the peak of the Chinese anti-Legion campaign, met some citizens of the new Republic in eastern Europe. He told them that their attack on Frank Duff, who had become an 'imperialist' in their propaganda, was a disgrace. 'He is a friend of mine,' said Peadar. 'If I was in trouble tomorrow, he's the man I would first turn to.' The result of this unscripted dialogue was an invitation to Frank to go personally to Peking! On another occasion he was invited to Moscow. Some day we shall know all the amazing things that happened to him and learn of his emotions in certain moments, for example, when the Legion was founded in Nazareth!

I have indirectly opened up one vast challenge which the Legion and its guiding spirit faced during the thirties and forties: expansion in the missionary territories of the Church. It has been said that the Catholic Church won the First World War without firing a shot. Why? Because of the changing political configuration in which we have latterly come to call the 'Third World'. Native peoples welcomed the faith and in places were baptised in large numbers. Africa is the prize example. Against the few thousand Catholics in the vast continent at the beginning of the century there are today over 30 million with a growing native clergy and episcopate, and all that a flourishing Christianity should possess.

It might have been tempting for a new lay association in a European country to leave the missions to the missionaries, but Frank Duff was never afraid to think big. In no time he was sending envoys to the dispersed messengers of the Good News, with astonishing results, as those who have followed the story of the Legion in Asia, Africa, Latin America know very well. It is true to say that there are many distant places on the world map where Ireland conjures up one only word, the Legion of Mary. This was the only truly international movement launched from our country.

I once had a piquant example of this. I was talking

to some American Franciscans who were preparing a special magazine feature on Frank. By way of interest I showed them some letters written by him to Alfie Lambe. Opened at random, they proved to be concerned with the possibility of extension in the Falklands. We were all impressed, as the Falklands campaign was just then in the news. No wonder people were impressed by Frank's knowledge of geography; places on the map had meaning for him in terms of the work to which he had dedicated his life. It was a long life, not only striking because he survived two attacks on his person with lethal weapons in his last years, one of which left him streaming with blood, but because he had been so indifferent to rules of health. He needed sleep; some do not need so much; but he, though needing it would often drive himself to action into the early hours. He once said that on a few occasions he had reached four o'clock in the morning without having the time to say his breviary, a lifelong habit – from the old Latin breviary which took more than an hour. On these occasions he would recite the whole office for the day before taking the rest for which his being ached. His day always included attendance at two Masses.

Yes, an extraordinary man; a sharp mind, an ability to assess situations accurately, singling out the spot where effort would have its highest result. Consider the Patrician movement, consider the *Peregrinatio*, without mentioning the hostel system on which the initial success of the whole organisation was built.

Who said, or should have said: 'Ideas without practice are barren, practice without ideas is blind?' It suits the life on which I am reflecting. This man had profound vision. He had the wisdom to know how vision must be given body; and then he had tenacity. He never let up. He went on right to the end of the road. He might meet insuperable barriers, as did the Mercier Society which was a stroke of spiritual genius – the first inter-faith association in our country since the Reformation, and the Pillar of Fire Society, founded at a time when Jews everywhere welcomed brotherly support, also doomed to run into an ecclesiastical roadblock. But Frank was ready to take up where he had been forced to halt, for, though he could be acid in criticism, the whole trust of his being was creative and constructive.

Was he a saint? Not plaster-cast, not a holy Joe, though he prayed enormously. He was tough, terribly tough, not a macho type, but virile in the essential meaning of the word. I heard him say with relish that once a drunken sailor pulled a knife on him at the door of the Morning Star hostel, 'but I had a large bunch of keys in my hand and I got in first. I got him on the mouth and floored him.' I don't suppose this will figure in the analysis of his virtue, in the preliminaries for possible beatification! Nor will another incident, the telling of which he prefaced with the remark: 'Now you won't read this kind of thing in the lives of the saints!' An official threatened to appropriate the house which he had got from Mr Cosgrave, then Minister for Local Government and President of the Executive Council and in which the Santa Maria hostel was sited. Frank's reply was that he would stage the greatest eviction scene in Irish history with the barred hostel occupied by himself, the other legionaries and the inmates. They would use every weapon available and they would be dragged out of it screaming, himself like the captain leaving the ship, last of all. He heard no more of that threat.

Did he have faults? He certainly had a temper, but he would probably say that when active it was a case of just anger – it is one of the human passions. He was a wonderful raconteur and possibly embellished the bare record at times, though most of what he had to tell needed no embroidery. He had had a fascinating life; he was strong-willed and possibly at times self-willed, but without that strong will the work would have collapsed time after time under one onslaught or another. A man must be allowed some defects of his virtues.

To me Frank's virtues were on the heroic – I almost said homeric – scale. He was a wonderful friend, staunch, unquestioning, delicate when the call was for a sensitive approach, ready to fight for those he loved. To a dear friend to whom he gave a copy of Rembrandt's *Knight* he once said: 'You know I'm a fighter.' It was totally true. He never laid down his arms while the combat raged, and he knew that the crown of victory, imperishable, awaited him. Like all fighters he had moments of repose wherein he looked enchanting. Sean O'Sullivan caught something of this in his drawing, as he did of the keen intensity of the man.

Frank had such simplicity. He was no fool; he knew that he belonged to the ages. He knew that he principally had effected a mighty change in the mentality of the Catholic laity, and of the hierarchy towards them. His voluminous correspondence alone is unique in Irish history. Never again could a monumental work on Catholic theology appear without an article on the laity, because, as someone said facetiously, the laity did not exist when the multi-volume work was being planned! If the Second Vatican Council could issue a conciliar decree on the Lay Apostolate – something no previous such assembly had thought of doing, if Lay Auditors had their place in the assembly, if, in a word, it was recognised that Paul spoke to the laity when he said, 'You are the Body of Christ, that is the Church', then Frank Duff's intuition was amply justified, his initiatives proved right to the benefit of the entire Christian community, and of mankind. He was a prime mover in a mighty revolution.

He once said to me, 'I know I have been a channel of mighty things.' He said it in a matter-of-fact way. To a friend of mine who rebuked him for being too critical, he admitted that had he been faithful to all the graces he had received he could have been another St Bernard! That is the kind of self-criticism you get in the lives of the predestined. He had been faithful.

Did he wear a mask? He did wear his greatness unaffectedly. Was the bearing of an 'ordinary' man meant to veil this greatness? His sense of humour and his unforgettable laughter which was his restorative for frayed nerves, served also to distract people from the legend he embodied.

I commend Hilde Firtel's portrait of Our Lady's Shining Knight, serious, laughing, in moments tempestuous, courageous to the marrow of his bones. We shall not look on his like again. But what supreme good fortune to have known him, enjoyed his company, seen him at last receive the honour that was his due – though his native city did not offer its freedom to this, its greatest citizen. Yes, a prophet is not without honour save in his own country. God made him and threw away the mould. His memory will remain a giant in his hopes, in his achievement and in his prayer.

Michael O'Carroll, C.S.Sp.

Preface

A person standing directly in front of a high building does not get a comprehensive view of it. Only from a certain distance will he recognise its real size, its exact outline. Something similar may be said about men who mark their age and set signposts for the future. An attempt to sketch the life of Frank Duff is subject to certain limitations. The research needed on a life of over ninety years with countless repercussions throughout the world, would fill numerous thick volumes; it would be a lifelong task.

Only the future will show the full stature of this man and his influence on the life and development of the Catholic Church. The contemporaries and first followers of Francis of Assisi or Ignatius of Loyola, despite their enthusiasm and veneration for their founders, were probably unable to grasp their true greatness.

If in spite of all this I take upon myself the task of writing a biography of Frank Duff, this is because I have been asked to do so, first by the German-speaking members of the Legion of Mary in view of my long-standing friendship with their founder, and then by the Concilium Legionis in Dublin. I fully realise that this attempt can only be a preliminary venture which, I hope, will be followed by many other similar studies. I wish to acknowledge with gratitude the help of the numerous legionaries in Dublin, who freely and generously shared their recollection with me and helped me to locate documents. They will forgive me if I do not mention their names; there were so many that I am fearful of forgetting some. I could not have written the book without them.

Hilde Firtel, *Frankfurt-on-Main*

1. An Irish Family

In no other European country, perhaps with the exception of Poland, is patriotism so tightly connected with religious sentiment as in Ireland. This is possibly due to the fact that the oppression by neighbouring England was directed just as much against the Catholic faith as against political independence. Outside of Ireland little is known of the kind of discrimination to which Irish Catholics were for centuries subjected. The 'penal laws' enacted from the sixteenth to the eighteenth century decreed among other things that Catholics had neither franchise nor right to sit in parliament. They were not allowed to attend a university and were excluded from the professions and from trade. When a member of a Catholic family embraced the Protestant faith the entire family possessions became his. Only in the late eighteenth century were these laws somewhat mitigated; the oppression did not cease.

Insurrections by the tortured people, intermittent over 300 years, were repeatedly quashed. The insurrection which began in 1916 continued for four years when the British conferred on twenty-six counties of Ireland commonwealth status within the British Commonwealth of Nations and partitioned the six north-eastern counties from the rest of the country. This arrangement was not acceptable to a very large section of the Irish people and finally resulted in civil war in Ireland. After this dreadful holocaust the Free State government assumed authority over the twenty-six counties. Mr William T. Cosgrave was the first president of the Executive Council. In 1932 Eamon de Valera was elected, and having introduced in 1937 a new constitution, his party gradually cut away all the agreements made with the British. This led eventually to the declaration of the Republic by John A. Costello, then Prime Minister, when he was on a visit to Canada in 1949. Both Eamon de Valera and William T. Cosgrave as fighters for freedom had been imprisoned and sentenced to death; both had been reprieved.

Of course there were Irish who saw in the British crown the God-given authority to which the Christian owed allegiance and loyalty. But in whatever direction the inhabitants of Ireland were inclined, the passionate love of their country was common to them all. That was true for a young couple who were married in Dublin in the year 1888. John Duff, reputed to be 'the best-looking man in Dublin' led Letitia Susan Freehill to the altar. Both of them hailed from Trim, some twenty-five miles north of Dublin. John Duff was a civil servant and so was Letitia, or Letty as she was called. Her father had been a headmaster in Trim – the first Irishman who had been allowed to occupy that position. She herself had been the first Irish woman to pass the examination for entry to the Civil Service, which only shortly before had been opened to the female sex. At first she had been sent to London where she worked for several years. When this career was opened to women in Ireland, she was recalled. However, after her marriage the young woman had to relinquish her work. On 7 June 1889 their first son was born, and two days later received in baptism the names Francis Michael. It was Pentecost Sunday, the solemn feast of the Holy Spirit. May we in this date see an omen of the outstanding part the Holy Spirit was to play in the life of that child?

Letty gave birth to six more children of whom however two died very young. Four grew up with Frank: his brother John, sisters Isabel, Ailis and Sara Geraldine. The family life was a very happy one; there was great unity and love among the members. The parents gave their children from the beginning the example of a virile and cheerful faith. We do not know very much about Frank's early childhood. He himself lamented later on that as the last surviving member of his family he had no one to ask how particular events had come to pass. At any rate he was a lively, gay child with a strong penchant for sporting activities. At first he attended a private elementary school which was run by nuns. When the family moved to another part of the city he went for some years to Belvedere, a Jesuit college which was nearby. Finally he was sent to Blackrock College, a secondary school from which numerous prominent personalities have come, President de Valera among them. Frank got through every grade with distinction and won various prizes, one of them for the Irish language which had been neglected and almost forgotten in the course of the centuries. It was only spoken in a few western and south-western regions of Ireland. Frank was easily enthused for a movement to revive the language and soon acquired an excellent knowledge of it.

Although he loved to read and acquired an outstanding general culture, he was in no way what one could call a bookworm. Cycling was his passion from his early youth and he would always find time for a game of football. During such a match a ball hit him behind the ear with full force. 'I did not say anything about it at home,' he reported later on. 'At the time such things were not taken so seriously.' But one may assume that this accident was the cause of the deafness which befell him at a comparatively early age and gave him much trouble. At the age of nineteen Frank finished his education at Blackrock College, again with distinction, and applied for a position in the civil service – a natural step in view of his family tradition. For this he had to pass an examination and won his place in a nationwide competition. This young man was held in high hopes by his family.

Frank was of medium height, rather slight but wiry,

and of great muscular strength. This in later years surprised many an assailant who believed he could make short shrift of this little man. His grey eyes had a roguish expression at times, showing his sense of humour. He liked to laugh and was always in a mood to see and underline the funny side of a situation. He was also inclined to pranks and practical jokes, but he was never offensive in any way. He was a most promising young man.

2. Ascent – Interior and Exterior

Frank was given important tasks in the civil service, in the British era and after the establishment of the Free State government. He had worked on statistics. In the handing over from the British to the Irish authorities he was secretary to Sir Cornelius Gregg who set up the native civil service. He was for a brief while secretary to the national leader, Michael Collins. He served in the Department of Agriculture, and was later moved to the Department of Finance.

Zeal and loyalty in his working life was only one side of his striving for perfection. Long before he had found his real destiny in life he published a booklet *Can We Be Saints?* in which, like St Francis de Sales, he advised lay people on how to attain holiness. It would be interesting to find out how many thoughts contained in the bud in this work appear later on in the *Handbook* of the Legion of Mary. At any rate we may be sure that Frank gave no advice in this book which he himself had not tried out and followed. He advocated daily Mass and Communion. The latter was not yet the common custom. The Communion Decree of Pope St Pius X, in which he recommended the early, frequent and daily reception of the Blessed Sacrament had only appeared a few years before and it had not yet become the general practice.

To Frank Duff it was a matter of course never to start a day without the Holy Eucharist. Later in life he used to hear two Masses each day. But he felt impelled to do still more. In 1913, when he was twenty-four years old, he decided to say the Divine Office every day. This prayer was at the time very much longer than it is today. It was said in Latin and there were no translations. To say it in its entirety took an hour and a half.

A priest once asked Frank to what he attributed the great graces and successes that he had received in the course of his long life, and he replied: 'To the fact that never on a single day did I omit reading the Breviary.' One year after making this resolution he went for the first time to Lough Derg, known as 'St Patrick's Purgatory'. It is a penitential pilgrimage of three days' duration, probably unique in the world. The penitential exercises begin with a period of fasting. Later on the pilgrim takes only hard black bread and tea without milk. A vigil is held during the first night; the second night the participants sleep on hard plank beds. In between there is prayer and meditation; the Rosary and the Stations of the Cross are said several times during the day, and rounds of stony penitential 'beds' must be done in bare feet.

From then on Frank went to Lough Derg for 49 years on the August Bank Holiday, until illness prevented him. He did not find it easy: 'From one year to the other I like it less,' he wrote later to a friend.

One day an acquaintance of his tried to enthuse him for membership in the St Vincent de Paul Society, an association founded by the Frenchman Ozanam, specialising in works of charity. In Ireland this association was limited to men. The member sees his task as service to the poor, not as that of an official social assistant, but as a friend who wishes to convince them that they are not forgotten by the Lord and that the Church is not indifferent to their plight. Frank seems to have hesitated at first and finally joined the society more in order to oblige his friend than from real interest. But soon he felt gripped, especially by the indescribable poverty in his home town, something which one can hardly imagine today. So far in his sheltered bourgeois existence he had not come in close contact with such things. The members of the St Vincent de Paul Society met every week in Myra House, an old somewhat derelict building which at one time had been a bacon factory. A benefactress had given it to the Society as a gift. At first only one room had been repaired for meetings. Little by little as the Society's activities expanded other rooms and the large hall had been renovated. The Society's meetings began with prayer and spiritual reading. The minutes were taken and work was discussed. Frank's experience with the St Vincent de Paul Society was to prove important in the subsequent foundation of the Legion of Mary. It was the framework adopted from the beginning. The Society numbered outstanding personalities among its members and was very active and lively. Frank was impressed by the atmosphere and soon was among its most zealous members.

3. A Very Special Apostolate

Proselytism was spreading throughout Ireland in the nineteenth century. Normally the word means seeking conversions, but in Ireland it meant a well-planned campaign to exploit the material plight of the people in order to make them leave the Catholic faith. In a pastoral letter the Archbishop of Dublin enumerated no fewer than twenty-one associations which under the harmless designation of 'social assistance' used these shameful means; it was said that these were not all the groups at work. Free meals and free medical treatment were offered; people were placed in homes and received all sorts of other favours if they were willing to attend a Protestant service – at that time a grievous sin for a Catholic.

One day the conference of the St Vincent de Paul Society to which Frank belonged, received a letter from a certain Tom McCabe, a friend of Frank's father and a zealous member of the Society, in which he reproached the brethren with tolerating such a nest of proselytism in their immediate vicinity and with doing nothing about it. In 6½ Whitefriars Street every Sunday a free breakfast was offered, followed by a Protestant service. The President, whose name was Lennon, asked for volunteers to investigate the matter and Frank came forward. He and Lennon agreed to meet the following Sunday and examine the situation. Frank did not realise at the time what he was letting himself in for, but it was plenty! The next Sunday was a very cold day. At 7.30 in the morning our two heroes arrived on the scene and took up their position. Soon the first guests appeared – pale, ragged wretches. Whilst Frank's companion began a conversation with one of them, he counted the persons who entered. Then a woman approached him. 'Mr Duff,' she said (he must have already been a well-known figure in Dublin since he himself did not know her) 'if you want to undertake something in this matter you ought to talk to Mr Gabbett; he is standing over there.'

Frank saw a tall, heavy man with a fierce black moustache; with the collar of his overcoat turned up he looked quite formidable, almost forbidding. Upon Frank's question he first glared at him and then declared he could not look any longer at these goings-on and had decided to open a counter-institution the following Sunday. 'But that's wonderful,' exclaimed Frank. 'We are looking for exactly such a possibility. Naturally we do not think of any competition, but we would like to help you.' Whilst Gabbett mumbled something Frank's companion returned and reported that he had just received permission from the director of the school on the other side of the road to use his premises for such an enterprise. When he heard that Mr Gabbett had the same plan he offered in the name of the St Vincent de Paul Society to defray the expenses. 'Thanks, I can manage alone,' replied Gabbett. This was remarkable in that he was a shoemaker and in no way blessed with earthly goods; but evidently he had his pride. 'May we at least help with the work,' he was asked and after some hesitation Gabbett agreed.

The next Sunday a giant of a man barred the access to the 'guests' calling to 6½ Whitefriar Street, and directed them to the opposite side of the road. Frank and Lennon helped with the preparation and serving of breakfast and afterwards they washed the dishes and cleaned up the rooms. From then onward this happened every Sunday. Since there was no evening Mass at the time the helpers had to go to a very early Mass in order to start their work at 7.30 a.m. and then work all morning without taking any food. Lennon's health was not the best; soon he could not stand it any longer and dropped out. But Frank was tougher. Besides, he had struck up a friendship with Gabbett. 'He was a person,' Frank recounted later, 'whose like I had never before encountered. For him there existed only one thing: his faith. For this, no sacrifice was too big for him. But what he demanded from himself he also asked from others.'

Frank worked at his civil service job until 5 p.m. Then he would, almost every day, visit people's homes in the service of the St Vincent Society. When it got so late that he could not very well ring at the door of strangers, he would drop in on Gabbett. As has already been said, he was a shoemaker and he had specialised in officers' boots which in those days was a handcraft. Even at this late hour he was regularly sitting over his work, and while the boot grew under his skilful hands he would talk without interruption and always on religious subjects. Gabbett belonged to the Pioneer Total Abstinence Association, the members of which for the love of Christ and in atonement for the vice of alcoholism bind themselves to lifelong abstinence from alcoholic drink, and wear a small badge as a sign of their membership. Gabbett won his young friend to the idea. Contrary to the later development of his mentor, Frank remained faithful to the promise throughout his life.

Gabbett could only write his name, but he was able to read and was very happy that Frank frequently made him gifts of religious books. The rooms where Sunday breakfast was now being offered stood empty during the week, which seemed a pity. So the two friends started all sorts of activities in order to avail themselves of the premises at other times. Frank held catechism classes for boys and men. Soon he recruited women and girls to give religious instruction to school girls. The year 1916 brought the insurrection which led to the war of independence, but that did not have Gabbett's sympathy. He had served in the British army in India for twenty-one years and considered himself a loyal subject of His Majesty the King of England. So he decided to join the British army again, although he had already passed the age of active service. It was typical of this strange man that he did not breathe a word of it in advance to his young friend.

Frank was in no way enthusiastic when one day Gabbett told him that he had given notice to the landlord of the place and was going to be a soldier once more. 'All you see in this room is yours,' he declared, and that was that. Frank took plates, cups, pots, cutlery and clothes to Myra House. Among all the odds and ends there was a painted plaster statue of the Mediatrix of Graces. Frank was to meet that statue again.

4. The Local Madman

If we follow Frank Duff's life from the beginning we can only state with admiration how Divine Providence educated and prepared him step by step for his great mission. We have seen how the young civil servant grasped the striving for personal sanctification as a prerequisite for any fruitful apostolic activity and how, by daily reading of the breviary, he gave stability to his efforts. We have seen furthermore how in the zealous Dublin branch of the Society of St Vincent de Paul he found the framework which taught him the value of regular organised activity within a group. He still had to learn to overcome human respect and not let himself be diverted either by derision or by violence from the path that led to his desired goal.

After Gabbett had joined the army and left his friend to himself, the breakfast place closed down and the callers turned again to the enterprise on the other side of the road. Frank found this intolerable and decided to continue picketing the place. Every Sunday he would pace up and down in front of the premises, Rosary in hand. If someone wanted to enter he would approach him and courteously explain that he was doing wrong. The response was nearly always the same: 'I am hungry.' Mostly the answer was given in a friendly tone, but on occasion ungraciously and rudely. The matter caused him profound disquiet. Then he got to know, not very far from the site of his efforts, a public soup-kitchen, directed by a priest, offering cheap meals during the week, but not on Sundays. Frank contacted the priest and convinced him of the necessity to open his kitchen also on Sundays. The priest declared his willingness to offer a breakfast at 3d per person. Today one cannot even buy a postcard for that amount, but at the time the sum did count, and Frank promised to pay the bill himself every week. He took up his post in Whitefriars Street again and handed to each person who was willing to go elsewhere, a card with his initials which would entitle him to a free breakfast in the soup-kitchen.

In the course of this activity he met with various adventures. One Sunday a drunken sailor appeared. Frank stopped him and said: 'If you are a Catholic it is wrong to enter a place where you are bound to attend a Protestant service.' Instead of a reply the sailor drew a knife and lunged at Frank – 'he would have killed me had he been sober,' Frank recounted later on – 'but being drunk he tottered so much that the blow missed me.' Frank was not only fearless, but he was not an easy man to deal with. 'My retort would have done very good credit to Muhammed Ali because it flattened him out,' he reported laughing. Whilst he prepared to meet a possible further attack a resolute lady who had watched the scene from the other side of the road threw herself at the man and beat and kicked him until he withdrew. Adventures of this kind were not infrequent, but nevertheless Sunday after Sunday Frank would pace up and down in front of the place and if no one was about he would say his Rosary.

One day a priest came with a group of young girls from a nearby church. He pointed at Frank and said in a tone loud enough for Frank to hear him: 'I just wanted to show you the local madman.' The girls giggled, but one bright young girl, knowing her Shakespeare, replied with the words of Polonius from *Hamlet*; 'There's method in his madness; you will see that in the end the place will close down.' This girl was Emma Colgan. In later years she was to play an important rôle in the Legion. At any rate, Emma was eventually proved right.

At this time Frank's father died, and as the oldest son

he had to help support his family. The weekly bill for the breakfast became too much for him. When at last he resorted to the St Vincent Society they agreed to pay the bill in the future. Not only that – a very fine man by the name of Tom Fallon, who was to play an important part in Frank's life, offered to help him picketing, which Frank accepted gratefully. From then onward there were new volunteers each week. In the end the place closed down but not for six and a half years after Frank's first intervention. It was no longer worth while keeping it open because the number of callers kept diminishing. Those responsible did not abandon their project as easily as that. On the other side of town there was a similar place, the Metropolitan Hall, and they decided to go there quietly. Evidently a little bird must have told the brethren of the St Vincent Society about this plan because, when on the next Sunday the new place opened its doors the faithful picketers were already on the spot, trying to convince the callers not to betray their faith for a breakfast. Soon afterwards Frank found other tasks which prevented him from picketing, but others took his place week after week, year after year, until the last of these places closed its doors. All in all the picketing lasted over sixteen years, but the madness had proved to have method.

5. Group Activity

It has often been pointed out that Our Lady appeared in Fatima in the year 1917 when communism came to power in Russia. Just as significant is the fact that in the same year the foundations were laid of a movement which decades later was to be denounced by the communists as 'public enemy number one'. But for the time being the grain of wheat was still hidden in the earth.

As has already been mentioned, Myra House had a

big hall in which free meals were distributed to destitute children on Sundays. Several women and girls helped regularly in this task. One day in the course of conversation with the children, a member of the St Vincent Society felt strong misgivings whether these little ones were really dependent on the free meals. When the parents were visited it appeared that some of them were not really destitute, so the free meals were discontinued. About this time Frank was appointed by the St Vincent de Paul Society to be its representative on the Ladies' Committee. This committee met monthly to organise various activities, the Pioneer Total Abstinence Society of the Sacred Heart being one of them.

For some time Frank had noticed a middle-aged woman who every day during lunch hour went to the Convent of Marie Reparatrice in Merrion Square. Her evident piety impressed him. One day he approached her and invited her to join the group. She accepted and introduced herself to Frank as Mrs Elizabeth Kirwan. Under her guidance a group of girls met monthly in Myra House to explain the idea of the Pioneers and other activities to interested persons. It included besides Mrs Kirwan several members of the St Vincent Society and some girls who formerly had helped in serving meals to the children. A zealous young priest, Fr Michael Toher, became spiritual director of the group. He was also director of the Conference of St Patrick of which Frank Duff was a member. Soon a warm friendship sprang up between him and the young priest.

It was now decided to establish a firm framework for the group meetings. After the opening prayers that were taken from the Society of St Vincent de Paul, the Rosary was recited. There followed a spiritual reading and the minutes of the previous meeting. Mostly the business of the Pioneers and other activities were quickly dealt with and each participant was then asked to report on what he or she had done in the service of God during the past month. The men usually visited homes on the work of the St Vincent de Paul Society, and the girls taught catechism. The little group was also available for any kind of help that might be needed. The meeting took place monthly and started at 4.30 p.m. At 6 o'clock the bells of the church on the opposite side of the road rang out the Angelus. That was the end of the meeting. Afterwards the ladies served the tea and started the social part of the evening, during which religious subjects were frequently informally discussed. That group first came together in 1917. One year later the First World War ended.

In 1919 Frank's old friend Gabbett returned from England. For a while he had done excellent apostolic work in the army. He had organised services for Catholic soldiers, brought back to the faith some who had given up the practice of religion and had gained some converts to the Catholic church. It was all the more suprising then that he now seemed to have lost his zeal. Not only had he given up all apostolic activity but he, who had won Frank to the Pioneers, had broken his pledge and started to drink. Frank was very disappointed. To one of Frank Duff's character, who, against all opposition, would stick to a way once he had recognised it as the right one, such behaviour was incomprehensible. 'What am I to do with him?' he asked two friends from the St Vincent Society to whom he had poured out his heart. 'Take him to Mount Melleray,' they advised. This was a Cistercian Abbey about seventy miles from Dublin, beautifully situated, which opened its gates to guests, offering them the opportunity to participate in the life and the prayers of the monks. Moreover it had the reputation of being able to cure alcoholics. Frank had always been a devotee of St Bernard, the founder of the Cistercians, and he willingly followed the advice. He was not disappointed. Gabbett was enthusiastic and found his way back to sobriety.

In Mount Melleray Frank had discovered his Tusculum. From that day onward there was not to be a single year without a visit to the Abbey; he went mostly in early summer. Later on he would bring friends and colleagues with him, so that at times a group of 30 or 40 guests visited the Abbey. This became such a firm usage that even after Frank's death the annual visits to Mount Melleray are being continued.

6. The Spark that Caught

In the evenings Frank went frequently to Myra House where he would always find something to do. Since most of the rooms had been renovated there was activity everywhere. There was hardly a day without meetings or conferences of some sort.

One evening Frank went into a room in which a man full of enthusiasm was commending a book to his listeners. Frank, always interested in books, stopped to listen. He neither knew the author, Louis-Marie Grignion de Montfort, nor his work. The discussion did not impress him, and soon he forgot all about it.

Frank loved reading. One may ask oneself how, with the pressure of his profession and unsalaried activities he found the time for it, but he was extremely well read. He was particularly well versed in English literature and always had quotations at his fingertips. One of his friends reports that once he took an entire afternoon off in order to read to her Coleridge's poem *The Ancient Mariner* which he loved, and which she did not know. No wonder then that he was a regular customer at the numerous second-hand bookshops and stands which at the time were to be found in Dublin. One day when he was browsing again through a display of books he found a small volume *The True Devotion to Our Lady* by Grignion de Montfort, translated into

English by Father Faber. Frank remembered that this was the work about which the man had been speaking so enthusiastically and since the price of four pence did not seem exorbitant to him, he bought the book and duly read it through.

Grignion teaches that Christ came into the world through Mary and that he works through her, that is, in the individual soul he is born by Mary and grows through her; and as it is said in the creed, this is always the work of the Holy Spirit. He who gives himself completely to Mary, who hands over to her all his temporal and spiritual possessions, who does everything with her, in her and for her, places himself therefore in the very floodstream of divine grace. Frank found the book exaggerated, even absurd, and put it on his shelf, thinking never again to open it.

Most Irish Catholics have a devotion to Our Lady – that is simply part of the Catholic faith. She is holy, probably the greatest of all saints, so one may ask her to intercede for us. One likes to sing the old Marian hymns, one may even recite the Rosary, but from there to the recognition of her unique role in the divine plan of redemption, to the complete giving of self to her, there is a long way – a way that Frank Duff had laboriously to seek and find. But the gospel saying about Jesus is also true about Mary: 'Not you have chosen me, but I have chosen you' and Mary always knows how to win those whom she has chosen. Frequently she uses human agents for this purpose.

Tom Fallon was a prominent civil servant and a leading member of the St Vincent de Paul Society. At an advanced age he was ordained a priest, and even in his ninety-fourth year worked successfully as a missionary in Mexico, but at that time he was still a layman. One day he asked Frank quite suddenly: 'Do you know De Montfort's *True Devotion to Mary?*'

'Yes, I have read the book.'

'And what do you think of it?'

'I don't like it.'

'Then you did not read it well.'

'Oh yes, I read it from beginning to end.'

'Perhaps, but not thoroughly enough. Perhaps you only skimmed through it. Read it again.'

Frank held Tom Fallon in high esteem and he obeyed – with the same result as the first time.

'Well, have you read the book once more?' Tom enquired at their next meeting.

'Yes, and I still find it exaggerated.'

Tom did not give in. Each time the two men met he would return to the subject.

'I do not recall how often this was repeated,' Frank wrote many years later, 'but it must have been half a dozen times.' One day he had a sudden illumination which he could only term as a special grace from God. He was struck by the realisation that the book taught the truth and that the fault had been his own – his lack of knowledge about Our Lady, his insufficient understanding of her role in the pattern of salvation.

The next step came again through an exterior impulse. As already mentioned Frank took his friend Gabbett to the Abbey of Mount Melleray in order to have him cured from his alcoholism. Having presented himself and his charge he was asked by the guest master whether he wanted something to read during his stay. It hit him like an electric shock. 'Yes, I am looking for a book about Mary,' he confessed – 'one that is really profound, but written clearly enough for me to understand it.' The guest master promised to look for such a work and shortly afterwards returned with a book by Joseph de Concilio. It was entitled *The Knowledge of Mary*. Frank began at once to read. He was gripped by the subject and felt with every line that this work would give him the knowledge for which he longed. The book runs to some three hundred pages, and at the time it was already out of print and probably not to be found anywhere outside the monastery. Thus

Frank decided – and that again is typical of him – to copy it. Every day he would write until all hours of the night. In this way the contents impressed themselves on his mind much more effectively than would have been the case had he merely read the book. Now Frank understood what Mary wanted to tell him. Later he expressed his thanks to the author by quoting a passage from the work in the Legion *Handbook*.

Frank was an apostle; if he discovered a treasure he must make it accessible also to others. The group meetings in Myra House seemed to be a particularly suitable one. Mrs Kirwan, and also some of the girls, might be interested. A person being confronted for the first time with De Montfort's thoughts frequently finds them exaggerated, or at least feels them to be a challenge, but there is also the feeling that 'there is something in it'. After Frank's introduction of the subject *The True Devotion to Mary* was frequently discussed by the group.

Some of the group were soon won over to it, others were still full of questions and doubts. One day a special meeting was fixed to which all interested persons were invited. It is not possible to establish with certainty when exactly this meeting took place. Probably it was in the month of August 1921. The entire evening was devoted to a discussion and explanation of the doctrine of Blessed Louis-Marie Grignion de Montfort – he had not been canonised as yet – and when the participants separated all of them had decided to adopt the True Devotion. 'It was as if an electric contact were established' one of the participants wrote later – 'and then something happens.' Very soon something happened indeed. The spark had caught.

7. 7 September 1921

One fine Sunday Matt Murray – at the time caretaker of Myra House – reported to the usual meeting of the group about his visit to the women's ward of the Union Hospital which he had made with another brother of the St Vincent Society. This was a hospital for the poor. His report was heart-rending. It would not be easy to find so much material and spiritual misery elsewhere. The section for cancer patients was especially bad; the women were rotting away. Visitors would shy away from the intolerable stench. This visit was an exceptional one because usually the brethren of the St Vincent Society visited the men's section of the hospital only. When after the Angelus the members were having their tea someone asked: 'Could not the girls regularly visit the women's section and the brothers go to the men?' The proposal was approved by all.

'On whom can we count?' was the next question. Six girls volunteered. 'So when may we meet?' The following Wednesday seemed to be suitable, and it was agreed to meet at 8 p.m. 'Try to bring along some friends!' Mrs Kirwan agreed to accept the presidency of the new group. Fr Toher, always kindhearted and helpful, was to be Spiritual Director.

When the participants appeared the following Wednesday – they had made every effort to recruit friends and there were fifteen people – they were surprised to find a small altar of Our Lady on the table. The statue of the Mediatrix had been among the things that Frank had got from Gabbett when the latter relinquished his premises to join the army. For years it had been standing around unnoticed in Myra House, but now it was standing on the table on a white cloth, flanked by two vases with flowers and two lighted candles. None of them, not even Frank suspected at that moment what was in the offing, only Mary knew. For a long time it was not known who had that idea about the statue, but years later it appeared that it had been Alice Keogh, a girl who later on became a nun.

The Holy Spirit was invoked and the Rosary was said; then they discussed the work to be undertaken. It was decided to hold a weekly meeting; the first work was to be visitation of the Union Hospital and it was to be done in pairs. For the time being no men were to join the group with the exception of Frank, who had been the driving force from the beginning, nor was material help to be given. Both these provisions were taken in consideration of the St Vincent de Paul Society. One could not very well snatch away their members, and material assistance was their characteristic task.

The minutes of that first meeting are still in existence and give an interesting insight. The secretary who had been elected had put Frank's name first on the list of participants. But this name was crossed out and at the end of the page we read in Frank's own handwriting: 'Frank Duff also took part in the meeting.' He always tried to conceal, or at least to play down his role in the foundation. Even in later years he did not like being called the founder of the Legion. The members agreed to see people as if Our Lady were going to visit them and see her Divine Son in each of them. When the work was allocated they almost quarrelled because everybody wanted to go to the cancer ward. Frank pricked his ears. Normally people tried to avoid disagreeable or difficult tasks, but here the contrary was the case, despite the fact that the members were mainly inexperienced young girls. The only one who had reached a mature age was Mrs Kirwan. She was very strict with her young charges who nevertheless respected and loved her. She was very poor, certainly the poorest of them all, and seemed to live entirely for God. It was she who soon afterwards introduced the custom of reading out once a month the four fundamental requirements of work in the new movement.

The Union Hospital was run by the Sisters of Mercy. When they heard of the new group and its aims they promised to offer Mass and Communion for its prosperity. As a kind of return gift the group chose for itself the name 'Association of Our Lady of Mercy'.

Several years afterwards the necessity was felt for some written records about the movement which in the meantime had grown remarkably. The date of its foundation was to be given, but no one remembered it.

'Now when was that?' the members asked each other.

'1921 naturally, but which month?'

'It must have been at the beginning of September.'

Finally they consulted the old book of minutes which Frank had prudently kept. The date of the first meeting was 7 September. 'What a pity!' someone remarked, 'the eighth would have been much more suitable – Mary's nativity and commencement of the Legion of Mary!' (In the meantime the movement had adopted this name). But Frank saw deeper. He was liturgically experienced as he read the Breviary every day and he possessed a special gift for detecting connections which could only be supernaturally explained. On 7 September at 8 p.m. the Church recited the first vespers of the Marian feast. On 8 September at 8 p.m. the feast has passed – the office of the next day is already impending. Mary's Legion was to be born with the opening prayers of her own birthday.

8. And Suddenly it Happened

At a second meeting, Frank Duff relates, everything went like clockwork. The reports were more than encouraging. The poor patients in the Union Hospital were happy about the visits and expressed their gratitude in eloquent and frequently touching terms. The minute book shows that each week new members joined the group. Only a few months after the foundation we read of about seventy sisters being present and we can only ask ourselves how each of them could give a report about the work performed – but the minutes say so explicitly.

Frank took part in every meeting. He understood with a kind of inner light that under his eyes something was growing which heretofore he had not known. He was conscious that Our Lady had taken the helm from his hands and now was herself leading the small band. But he knew equally well that complete and unconditional giving of self was demanded from him and from the other members. One day about three months after the birth of the new movement its future was being discussed. Then and there Frank predicted that it was to spread over the whole world. This struck the girls as being so funny that they burst into hearty laughter. 'They laughed for at least five minutes,' Frank recounted later. 'That shows what they thought of my gift of prophecy.'

A long time before the group came into existence Frank had been thinking about the plight of the Dublin street girls, and what he could do about it. In the course of an errand in the service of the St Vincent de Paul Society, he had one day entered a house which lay on his way. Suddenly he realised it was a lodging house for prostitutes. He had never entered such a building before and he retreated in panic. Since then the problem often occurred to him. He thought of opening a cheap lodging house for street girls which could be run by some pious women, but for the time being these were just castles in the air. Of course several convents of the Good Shepherd sisters existed in Dublin where prostitutes who wanted to change their way of life could enter as 'Magdalens', but it was a very rare occurrence for a girl to come spontaneously. The nuns were sitting in their convents waiting for candidates; they did not go out to search for them.

About eight or nine months after the start of his apostolic group Frank received a letter from a nun with whom he was acquainted. She had met two middle-aged ladies who appeared to her as being well suited for apostolic work and she wanted them to work with Frank. Both of them were enthusiastic about joining the foreign missions and had offered themselves to a missionary order. The reply had been 'too old'. They had been making plans on how to help the missions in other ways. So when Frank told them about his idea of a lodging house they were struck by it and declared themselves willing to live in such a house and care for the inmates. The first branch of the Legion had too many members already and there was also different work to be done, so a second branch came into being almost by itself. The young plant had got its first offshoot. Then Our Lady took things into her own hands once more. The new branch had only met twice when a mission for the women of the Francis Street parish was held. The missionary, a young Passionist priest, visited the families with a young curate of the parish, and entered the house from which Frank had once fled so hastily. Thirty-one street girls lived there. The two priests called them together and appealed to their conscience. To their surprise they found the girls in no way hardened and depraved as one often imagines prostitutes to be. On the contrary, many of them began to cry and declared that they would like to change their way of life but did not see any possibility. The young curate – his name was Fr Creedon – talked to the landlady and offered to pay her £4 a day if the girls were no longer forced to work at their profession. This was a generous offer but not a permanent solution. Frank called a meeting of all interested parties. Besides himself, the two new members with a companion and four priests took part. Feverishly they were looking for a solution. One of the priests present, Fr Devane, had recently opened a retreat house for men and considered a closed retreat as a kind of panacea. Extraordinary as it seemed, the proposal of winning the thirty-one girls, for a retreat was accepted 'as a drowning man will catch at a straw' – as Frank described it. But before the idea could be put to the girls suitable premises had to be found. Fr Devane with one of the ladies made the round of all Dublin retreat houses but everywhere they met with a shocked refusal. Finally, the Mother Superior of a convent outside Dublin agreed to put their school at the disposal of the girls – it happened to be holiday time – if they brought along their own beds. However, she had first to seek the permission of the Mother General.

Now, here is one of the astonishing details which accompanied the progress of the young association from its beginning: the Mother General said 'No'. That was in the year 1922, in the midst of the Civil War. A saboteur cut the telephone wire at exactly the right moment and the refusal could not be heard.

Next, the girls must be won to the idea. The entire strength of the second branch of the Legion was devoted to this task. Within a few days the field of work of the young movement was extended from the relatively easy and beautiful task of visiting the sick, to the very difficult one of apostolic work for the derelicts of society.

9. The Incredible Venture

Frank Duff has described the extraordinary events that followed in a number of articles which appeared in serial form in the bulletin *Maria Legionis,* started fifteen years later. Still later they were assembled in a book entitled *Miracles on Tap* and I do not wish to repeat them here in detail.

Frank liked to tell his visitors about those exciting times. He had an excellent memory, and especially the astonishing happenings of the next two years had profoundly engraved themselves in all their details on his mind. Whoever heard him speak about the events that followed in rapid succession will never forget it.

Frank's days had been full for a long time because of his professional and apostolic work, but what occurred now plunged him into a whirlpool of activity which would have killed a weaker person. It was about this time too that he was transferred to the Ministry of Finance and the young civil servant found himself on the upward promotional path. Now there followed what in Frank's own terms was the 'unprecedented retreat'. Five members had the task – in no way easy – to win the girls in that house to the idea; then a retreat master had to be found – and all at the shortest possible notice. Finally beds had to be bought – on credit, because there was no money. 'What a crazy idea! It will make you look like fools!' many well-meaning people warned. Contrary to all pessimistic predictions, twenty-three of the thirty-one girls appeared punctually at the appointed meeting place and they were taken in a bus that Frank had rented to the convent at Baldoyle.

Only the Mother Superior knew what kind of people she had taken in. The other nuns were left in the belief in writing what they wanted. He would present the matter at the Cabinet meeting which was to be held that very evening. The petitioners were asked to call again the next day. They did so and were handed a letter – which today is hanging in a frame in the Legion Headquarters in Dublin – which said that a building in Harcourt Street in the very heart of the city was put at their disposal free of rent for a period of three months. Thus Frank was able to return to Baldoyle and joyfully announce that he had found lodgings for all the girls. The retreat master spent the whole day hearing the girls' confessions.

During the following night Frank had no sleep. Together with Father Philip, the retreat master, he paced up and down for hours in the convent garden and discussed again and again the miraculous draught of fishes that had been granted to them. Next morning all the girls with the exception of two non-Catholics received Holy Communion. As usual Frank was kneeling in the last pew and looked on as one after the other went up to the altar. He now knew each one of them and for each one he had been praying and worrying. 'I can say without hesitation,' he wrote later on 'that this was the most wonderful Mass I ever heard'.

It was necessary to prepare the house for the new occupants. Beds were at hand, but there was no other furniture nor the money to buy it. Frank however was not the person to give up so near his goal. He went straight to his old friend Gabbett whom he found as usual working away in his shoemaker's shop. 'You must help me!' he said and Gabbett agreed immediately. The friends rented a four-wheeled horse-dray and went with it to Myra House, where to the dismay of the doorkeeper they began to ransack the rooms. Tables, chairs, benches, cupboards, everything was loaded onto the horse-dray until it was full – a procedure in which Gabbett's enormous physical strength was a great help. It must be recorded to the eternal glory of that the girls belonged to an association of the Sacred Heart. Of course there were some moments of anxiety throughout the retreat when it was feared that one or the other of the retreatants – or all of them together – would run away. But nothing of the kind occurred; the girls followed the retreat to the end and all of them declared that they were willing to change their lives. All but two of them went to confession – they were not Catholics but expressed the wish to be received into the Church. One girl had formally apostasised. In order that she might be received back into the Church the Bishop's permission was required. As will be remembered, the telephone wires had been cut, so Frank rushed into the City and met the Vicar-General at the very moment when the latter was about to take a tram to his living quarters. The Vicar-General was surprised to be approached on the sidewalk by a breathless young man and asked for the necessary permission. He granted it, but with the pious admonition to choose a less extraordinary way the next time.

On the second day of the retreat Frank understood that the Lord was preparing for him a truly miraculous draught of fishes. Should the girls now be allowed to return to their former lodgings? If so, one might as well have spared oneself the entire effort. But where to find housing for twenty-three girls in a big city? Financial means were lacking as well. After a lengthy discussion it was decided that only the Government could help in this case. In the company of Fathers Creedon and Devane, Frank went to the Ministry of Local Government and asked to see William T. Cosgrave, later to become head of the government. Their wish was granted. The three petitioners presented their request. Mr Cosgrave got quite excited. Like a lion in his cage he paced up and down in the room. 'I don't know what to do but I know that I must do something,' he declared. After further deliberation he placed a sheet of notepaper before Frank and asked him to set down the St Vincent de Paul Society that they shortly afterwards made a gift to Frank of the entire furniture he had carried off, and even added a cheque for £5 for the purchase of other necessary items.

In the meantime the girls had returned from the retreat. They vied with each other scrubbing and cleaning and soon the place was spick and span. Then the furniture van arrived with the beds, and shortly afterwards the horse-dray with the other furniture. In a few hours the whole house was changed into a cosy hostel. It was named 'Sancta Maria'.

In Myra House Frank had found an old statue of the Sacred Heart. It was among the articles that Gabbett had left him before going to England. Now it was set up in the parlour of the new hostel, and the very same evening Fr Creedon proceeded to the enthronement of the Sacred Heart in the presence of all the new occupants of the house. What happened within a few days bordered on the miraculous. One fact must still be noted which can be found again and again in Frank's whole life: helpers were always sent to him at the right moment.

Frank never could have undertaken the venture of opening such a hostel were it not for the two ladies whom Frank had met only a few weeks before and who were willing to live as indoor sisters in the hostel with the girls. They too had found their real mission after much searching and doubting. Frank found himself with responsibilities that had grown alarmingly, but he possessed gigantic strength. With the help of his Heavenly Mother he was able to shoulder this new responsibility as well.

10. Assault on the Devil's Stronghold

There followed a period of comparative peace and consolidation. The 'miraculous draught of fishes' continued to show its beneficial consequences; several girls were able to find jobs, others got married or returned to their families. The legionaries started approaching other street girls in the city and inviting them to change their lives and enter the hostel. Soon another retreat was held. In the long run, as it was difficult to find suitable houses it was decided to hold the retreats in the Sancta Maria hostel. The latter became so well known that at times girls would present themselves of their own volition and ask to be admitted. In the meantime the membership of the first branch of the Legion grew so rapidly that another one was formed from it – the third in the young movement – and soon a fourth.

One day a report written in the minutes of the Sancta Maria branch proved to be a bombshell: two girls had left the hostel and had vanished from sight. They had gone to Bentley Place. This city quarter had a deplorable reputation throughout Europe. As bad as London's Soho or Hamburg's Reeperbahn, it had become a hotbed of vice and crime. As prostitution was forbidden by law in Ireland, the houses which the legionaries usually visited were not brothels, but just private lodgings of the street girls. In Bentley Place however there were brothels, and to this was added illegal selling of alcoholic liquor and other forbidden practices. Whoever entered as a client and dared to oppose some local custom could reckon with all sorts of unpleasant experiences. The prostitutes in the quarter robbed, plundered and despoiled every client, and woe to those who dared to protest. A Dublin police chief had once tried to clear out the quarter but had failed miserably. Since then things were just allowed to run their course. The police closed both eyes as 'nothing could be done about it'. There were terrible rumours about persons who had been beaten past recognition, about corpses that had been hurriedly buried somewhere at dawn. And now two girls from the Sancta Maria hostel had gone to that place. They were sure that they would be left in peace there, but they had not reckoned with the apostolic spirit of Frank Duff and his helpers.

At first it was just discussed, but soon the thought of venturing into the place was seriously considered. Finally the legionaries arrived at the conclusion that there would be little sense in converting the street girls of Dublin if this plague spot was allowed to continue in existence.

Frank Duff's description of the events that followed is more breath-taking to read than any thriller, particularly as it is the truth. Today, after so many years all this is history. People will say 'wonderful' and then forget about it, but at the time it was a decision demanding heroism. Frank himself formulated it thus: 'Here lies your duty and your destruction'. Think what people would undergo if it were a matter of rescuing persons from a burning house, saving lost mountaineers or salvaging the shipwrecked! but when it is *only* a matter of souls, should one rest on one's oars and leave everything as it is? It was decided to penetrate into Bentley Place. (By the way, this was not the real name of the district, but an assumed one that Frank had invented when years later he described the campaign; he did not want to embarrass its new inhabitants).

It was an heroic decision, but it was not taken with shouts of 'hurrah'. The helpers had been told that they might be killed or at least maimed in there. It was no shame to be afraid, for with a few exceptions they were just young girls who, after Frank had made the initial incursion with a companion, were sent week after week into this nest of Satan. Although there were many moments of danger in which martyrdom seemed to be disquietingly near, not one of the helpers actually came to harm. Many things turned out to be gross exaggerations and sometimes mere rumours. There were however plenty of horrors in the place. Although the narcotics of our day were not yet known, the people there drank methylated spirit, a poison which not only creates the same addiction as does heroin, but which destroys the human personality even more quickly and thoroughly than the latter. There were human wrecks, tattered and filthy, whose mere appearance made one shudder. One met pimps and bullies, who did not hesitate to beat a person to a pulp. The owners and profiteers of the brothels, those who in reality pulled the wires, were never seen.

Eventually this venture was quite successful. At any rate there was an unexpected string of conversions and many girls left Bentley Place to start a new life in the Sancta Maria hostel.

Of the numerous adventures and highlights which Frank Duff recounts in his report I would like to mention two. There was the episode that has found its way into the Legion *Handbook,* when Frank once was pressed by a colleague in the office to admit that most of his charges were hopeless cases he finally confessed almost reluctantly that he knew only one girl whom he considered as hopeless. This girl was converted the same evening and never relapsed into her former life. The second episode concerns a 'burglary' that Frank committed. A prostitute had promised to enter the hostel and had made an appointment with Frank and his helpers for a certain hour. When the legionaries appeared they found the house seemingly empty and all the doors blocked up. However, as Frank had good reason to suspect that the girl was at home, he lifted the shutter which covered a large window; then he succeeded in opening the window and climbing into the house. On the first floor he found the girl together with a friend, but she did not want to keep her promise and steadfastly refused to come along. Frank's good words did not have any effect, until suddenly her friend, who was not a Catholic, said: 'Well if you don't go, I will.' This woman was known as Manchester May after her birthplace. A few weeks later she was received into the Church and returned to her family. How many burglaries are committed daily, hourly, in order to get at jewellery or money! Why should one not risk such a deed in order to save an immortal soul?

After two years of patient endeavour one of those happenings which led the course of things in an apparently providential direction occurred once more. In the parish where Bentley Place was situated, a mission was held. This seemed to be a good opportunity for a frontal attack on the scene of vice which was already showing signs of crumbling. At first a great campaign of prayer was organised to be undertaken by all four existing branches. The local residents were shown that it was their duty to take part in the crusade of prayer, and whilst the mission followed its beneficial course drawing large crowds, Frank with the missionaries sought the owners of the brothels in order to persuade them to close down their houses. There too they experienced a miracle: a number of them declared themselves willing to do so and they kept their promise. On a certain day all the brothels were to close. It would certainly have been too good to be true if everything had gone off smoothly, but naturally there were some who at the last moment hoped to profit from the closing down of the others and tried to blackmail Frank with demands of payment. Only a few broke their word. As will be remembered, the running of brothels was forbidden by law in Ireland – and the police were called in to occupy the remaining houses and put some of the recalcitrants behind bars. Anger and hatred flared up once more in the hearts of those still left behind and they openly threatened to kill Frank Duff and his helpers should they again venture into the district. If they had yielded to intimidation they might have forfeited the moral success of their enterprise. They were accustomed to making their rounds in there twice a week, and when the usual day came along they entered as if nothing had happened, but again, not one of them suffered the threatened martyrdom.

The empty houses were filled with poor families who, in view of the existing housing shortage, overcame their dislike of the ill-famed district. Later on most of the houses were pulled down to make room for new buildings. Thus a small group of determined persons had succeeded in blotting out a disgrace on their town, which had existed for 150 years and against which the police had been powerless, and this had been done by gentleness and charity.

One certainly has to admit that the entire happening seemed like a miracle, but Frank had got used to expecting miracles. If the Church is the living Christ, then miracles belong to her everyday life, as miracles and signs were an essential part of the life of Christ. But of course man has to give everything; he must go to the utmost limit of his ability and his devotion. When he reaches this he acquires, so to speak, a claim on God's almighty intervention. Anybody can therefore obtain miracles if he is willing to pay the price for them. From then onward Frank Duff acted consciously according to this principle, and he was never disappointed.

11. A Movement takes Shape

If we consider the personality of Frank Duff we cannot help asking ourselves if he was a mystic. He certainly was not one in the sense of visions, ecstasies and other extraordinary manifestations. He was even proud that the Legion of Mary had not come into being on the basis of apparitions (there are even persons who resent this fact). Nevertheless there are many things in his life which can only be described as mystic inspirations.

As we have seen, more branches of the new movement were coming into existence. Each one had chosen a name for itself. We may remember that the first one had been called *Our Lady of Mercy,* the second chose the name *Immaculate Conception,* the third was called *Our Lady of the Sacred Heart,* the fourth *Refuge of Sinners.* Now it became necessary to find a name for the entire movement – all the more so as the single branches were to be united under a central council. Finally a meeting of that council took place and the necessity of choosing a name was discussed. It was decided to hold a novena so that the right decision would be made, in which all the members would take part. At the next meeting various proposals were presented, each more unsuitable than the other. Frank had racked his brain just as his colleagues had done. He knew how much depended on a suitable name. Above all he was looking for a name that was not only short and concise but could also, with a slight change, be applied to the members.

On the eve of the second meeting Frank was in his study. It was very late, midnight had long passed, and Frank got up to go to bed. For a moment he paused in front of the large picture of Our Lady which adorned one wall of the room when suddenly in his mind the words seemed quite spontaneously to form themselves: THE LEGION OF MARY. With this every doubt vanished. The name not only characterised the movement, it could also be applied to each single member who became a legionary of Mary. We believe this to have been an authentic mystical experience – and it was not the only one of its kind in Frank's life. What a disappointment the next day when at the meeting Frank's proposal was rejected! The only consolation was the fact that the other names presented were deemed unsuitable as well, and it was suggested that another novena be held.

One month later the next meeting took place; again, many proposals were made. Frank did not say a word, and Fr Creedon addressed him: 'Have you not got any proposal?'

'I made one the last time, it was rejected, but I do not know a better one than The Legion of Mary.'

The proposal was unanimously accepted. That was in the month of November 1925.

Now Frank widened his thoughts. Legion! Had not that been the name of the Roman army? What a model of zeal, courage and obedience was this for the Legionaries of Mary who now set out to conquer the world for Christ as the ancient legionaries had conquered the world, as it was known at the time, for the Roman empire. Frank knew Latin and the daily recitation of the breviary kept him in practice. What did the Roman legionaries call their garrisons? Yes, Praesidia. From now onward this should be the name for the single branches of the Legion of Mary. The use of Latin had the advantage that the various Legion units could bear the same name in all countries, so that translations into the various languages became unnecessary. Something else resulted from the idea of the Roman Legions. Each one of them had their standard which underneath the picture of the Roman eagle showed the portrait of the commander-in-chief in a medallion. What was more obvious than to design an emblem for the Legion of Mary after that model! The eagle was replaced by the dove – symbol of the Holy Spirit, and the commander-in-chief was Our Lady. The picture of the Mediatrix as it appears on the miraculous medal offered itself for the purpose. Several drawings were made, they were criticised, improved upon – and eventually there emerged the 'Vexillum', the characteristic standard which graces the table at each meeting, which is carried as a banner in processions and which appears on the Legion notepaper and its publications. In a somewhat similar way Frank was enlightened about the Legion promise. It had appeared that before the final enrolment of the members a period of probation should intervene; its duration was by common accord fixed at three months. The enrolment was to be sealed by a promise which in condensed form should express the Legion's spirituality, because only persons who understood and accepted this spirituality were suitable for membership.

Frank happened to be at Mount Melleray once again and it was Whitsuntide. He was thinking about the promise and suddenly he knew that it was not to be addressed to Mary – but to the Holy Spirit. Not that the legionary turns away from Mary; on the contrary he is so-to-speak looking through her, and recognises in her action the Holy Spirit who has formed in her the historic Christ and continues to form through her the mystical Christ in the heart of each person.

Thus Frank formulated the legion promise – a masterpiece in depth of thought and beauty of language – that promise which as Pope Paul VI was to declare many years later, had encouraged thousands of legionaries to accept responsibility of martyrdom. The Legion prayers too had been established in the meantime and received the *imprimatur*. Of particular beauty is the concluding prayer which in many respects reflects De Montfort's own words.

Next, a suitable picture was needed to adorn the prayer card, but not one of the numerous pictures which were considered appeared to be really adapted to the Legion. At the time a young artist by the name of Hubert McGoldrick was living in Dublin. He had already achieved a certain fame as an artist in stained glass. Frank was acquainted with the artist's two sisters who introduced him to their brother. After several discussions he painted the picture, which he presented to the Legion, and which now appears on the prayer card and on the *Handbook* cover. This picture not only reflects the Legion prayers; it also points very clearly to De Montfort's prophecy which Frank Duff, and the Legion created by him, dare to apply to themselves: 'This prospect lets me hope for a huge success, that is to say, for a legion of valiant and courageous soldiers of both sexes who in the dangerous times which are more than ever impending, will fight the world, the devil and depraved nature, rosary in their left, crucifix in their right hand.

By now the instruments were finished and ready. The conquest of the world could start.

12. The Burden is Growing

'How many divisions has the Pope?' Stalin is said to have once scornfully asked. Now, under Mary's motherly care an army was growing whose divisions years later were to be denounced as 'Public Enemy No. 1' by the red hordes. But, as a Chinese proverb says, a journey of a thousand miles starts with a single step. The number of praesidia had risen to thirteen, all of them still in Dublin. In the year 1927 the first branch outside the capital was started in Waterford. A year later Frank went to Scotland for negotiations about a beginning in that country. It was at once apparent that no written document existed to inform interested persons about the new movement. This was absolutely necessary if the Legion was to spread.

So Frank sat down and wrote. After a short account of the Legion's origin, its aims and its spirituality, he described rules and usages which during the past years had come into being almost by themselves. The resulting brochure got the title *Handbook of the Legion of Mary*.

Generally at the foundation of organisations and associations statutes are designed and recorded according to which the members work. Here the opposite way was chosen. The Legion had been at work for almost seven years without its rules having been set down in writing. The *Handbook* therefore was just to be a photographic image of the movement; it was only to record what had been practised for a long time. At first Frank undertook the trips to neighbouring countries when it was a matter of new beginnings. Here a special feature of the Legion appeared which has certainly promoted its worldwide extension. Although in each country the emphasis of the work was different, the system always proved to be so appropriate that it seemed planned to deal with the particular country's problems. For instance, there was a vast difference between the atmosphere of Catholic Ireland and the Scottish communities where the Legion gained entrance in the year 1928, and in England where a year later the first praesidium was started.

In the year 1930 an English legionary settled in India. A few months after her arrival she succeeded in starting a branch in Madras. Up to that time the Legion had been established in English-speaking countries only. In the year 1930 with a companion, Frank went to Paris and obtained the approval of Cardinal Verdier for the introduction of the Legion to France. That was exactly one hundred years after our Lady's apparition in the

Rue du Bac where she had charged the young postulant Catherine Labouré to have a medal of the Immaculate Conception struck, afterwards known as the Miraculous Medal. It was a strange coincidence. However, the practical introduction of the Legion into France took place more than ten years later. In the same year the Legion made the leap across the Atlantic and in the mining town of Raton in the State of New Mexico the first American praesidium came into being. It consisted of men only. From then onwards an ever-growing number of men flocked into the Legion.

In Dublin itself there were significant developments during that decade. The necessity appeared ever more urgent to create, analogous to the Sancta Maria hostel for street girls, a hostel for down-and-out men of whom there were hundreds in Dublin – unemployed tramps, alcoholics, jailbirds, who had hardly any prospect of rehabilitation unless they were effectively helped. But once Frank had recognised a necessity he did not rest until he had succeeded in meeting it. It would fill an entire book to describe in detail what work and effort it cost him to build up a second hostel. First he addressed a long letter to the Poor Law Commission set up in Dublin in which he described in stirring words the misery of these poor wretches and insisted on the necessity to offer them a possibility to re-integrate themselves into society. It was typical of Frank that he never contented himself with pointing out problems; he always proposed ways for their solution which seemed feasible to him (by-the-way, he demanded the same thing from his legionaries).

First of all he was clearly aware that the inmates of the projected hostel were not to be accepted gratuitously. They were to pay a modest contribution for their lodgings and board, and if they were completely destitute, work off their debts inside the hostel. 'Things that cost nothing are worth nothing' – and it would consciously or unconsciously raise their self-respect if they felt that they were themselves defraying the cost of their living. As a sequel to his written submission he was called several times before the Commission and subjected to a kind of cross-examination. Finally his determination won the day.

Another problem arose at once; where could one find suitable premises. In the end he remembered the old North Dublin Workhouse. The whole building was put in order by the combined efforts of the government of the day and by Frank and a number of his friends – bricklayers and carpenters, plumbers and electricians when they had finished their regular work, made a gift of the remaining hours of the day, their leisure hours, to Our Lady. 'Chartres Cathedral was built in this way,' says the writer Cecily Hallack in her book about the Legion of Mary. On 25 March 1927 the work was finished. The new hostel opened its doors under the name of 'Morning Star'. The same day the first two inmates moved in, and for the first time in many years slept in clean beds. Naturally it was important that a few members of the Legion were willing to move into the hostel themselves and run it. In the meantime hundreds of men were brought back to an ordered life by their stay.

Only in Heaven will it be known what effort, suffering, disappointments and difficulties this hostel cost Frank. 'It has been paid for by sweat and blood' are his own words.

Three years later a similar hostel was opened for unmarried mothers and homeless women. It was in the same block as the 'Morning Star' and bore the name 'Regina Coeli'. Again, a few of the first legionaries decided to move into the hostel and run it. In both hostels, one room was fitted out as a chapel. Mass and devotions were regularly held there. Here too the furnishing and decoration was done by the legionaries themselves. Years later permission was obtained to keep the Blessed Sacrament in both hostels. Several praesidia had the task of helping in the running and the care of the two hostels. Their members would appear in the late afternoon after their work, to help prepare and serve meals and to talk to the inmates. In one part of the Regina Coeli building the Legion office was housed – two or three small rooms, a couple of filing cabinets, a few typewriters. Fortunately Frank was able to rent a house which immediately adjoined the Regina Coeli hostel. There he moved with his mother, who now kept house for him, and his brother and sisters. The only luxury to which Frank treated himself was a dictaphone and here he dictated his correspondence, mostly late at night. With each country that the Legion of Mary conquered his task would grow and finally reach dimensions which defy description. He is said to have written more than one hundred thousand letters, and most of them were long. He also found himself with the responsibility for three hostels and all the burdens and problems connected with them. The running of one of them would have been sufficient to employ a person to full capacity. To this were added the every day tasks of the Legion of Mary which, as Frank once declared, was 'the apple of his eye'. It was about to conquer the five continents at an ever-growing pace.

13. The Sign of the Cross

Did the new movement which was so evidently blessed by God meet with unanimous enthusiasm? Unfortunately not, especially on the part of some of the clergy. Often it was openly rejected. The main reason for this was probably the fact that Frank was far ahead of his time – more than a quarter of a century before the Second Vatican Council which imposes the general duty on every Christian to be an apostle. It was not only Frank's conviction but also his experience that every baptised and confirmed person was not only called to evangelise, but also capable of it. Years later an *imprimatur* for a collection of articles by Frank Duff was refused on the grounds that he made a commandment of a mere counsel.

According to the opinion of numerous priests, lay people could at best be used as messengers. One could let them clean and adorn the church and keep the ecclesiastical vestments in order, but pastoral work was out. For this one had to study! This was the exact opposite of Frank's conviction. He believed that every convinced Catholic was capable of acting as an evangelist if he possessed a very simple picture of his faith. The work of the Legion itself was best learned according to the system of 'master and apprentice', that is to say, from an experienced legionary. If legionaries were asked to frequent instruction classes there would be very few prepared to persevere, and work in the mission countries would become absolutely impossible. It also must be said with regret that at times jealousy and the struggle for power were at the root of the resistance to the new movement. There was one particular order in the Church which fought the Legion with its whole might, for years – so much so that on one occasion in a large Asian country the Papal Nuncio called the local Provincial and implored him not to obstruct evangelisation in a mission land! We could quote many more sad examples of hostility towards the Legion, but we will refrain from doing so, firstly because numerous members, even of the order referred to, helped the Legion against the explicit instructions of their superiors; secondly because it was just this stubborn resistance which frequently contributed to making the Legion known, and above all because these stories belong to the past and there is little point in causing ill feeling today by raking up such sad events. This opposition often made Frank's life terribly hard. Added to this was the steadily growing burden of the civil service. As there were few men of his capability in the Department of Finance his career continued to move upwards.

The Legion of Mary was now receiving worldwide recognition. Frank had many enthusiastic helpers, but not one of them was able to take an over-all look at things as he could. Often he would return home at midnight completely exhausted. He would sit down in an armchair and fall asleep. Only after a couple of hours was he able to start reading his breviary. Soon this life seemed intolerable. He felt he would break down under the double burden and resented the time taken up by his job. His confessor however advised him not to relinquish this for the time being because the future seemed too uncertain.

The Second Vatican Council has brought ecumenical dialogue into the light of general consciousness. Frank Duff anticipated this dialogue by many years, but here too his way was blocked. In 1941 he started an association in Dublin named 'The Mercier Society' after the ecumenically-minded Cardinal Mercier, which fostered dialogue between members of different Christian communions. In an atmosphere of fraternal charity, Catholics, Protestants of the various shades, clerics and laymen would meet. One subject was treated at each meeting and, after the opening talk, discussion followed. Frank would, with his keen intellect often bring up quite new and surprising ways of seeing things. Although he never offended against Christian charity he disliked nothing as much as the syncretism against which Pope Paul VI was later to warn Catholics. The truth can be a victim of so-called love of one's fellowmen. Frank never wavered in regard to truth once he recognised it. He never put a personal opinion above the teaching of the Church, but he was so firm in his convictions that his partners respected and esteemed him, which was to be seen in the popularity of the Mercier Society and the steadily growing number of its members. Then one day all that ended. The Mercier Society was abruptly forbidden. It is not always easy to be in advance of one's time. A similar fate befell the society founded for dialogue with Jews, the Pillar of Fire Society, which had been supported by leading Dublin Jews.

14. With Pope Pius XI

As Frank was faced on all sides by ever-growing difficulties the thought gradually grew in him that he should apply for help to Rome. He knew the Most Rev. Paschal Robinson, OFM, the Nuncio Apostolic to Ireland, and asked him for his advice, but even there he was not encouraged. How would the Pope receive an unknown layman who simply appeared in Rome without any recommendation by his bishop? At that time Cardinal Marchetti heard about the Legion from Fr Hayes (later Canon Hayes, Founder of *Muintir na Tire*) and asked if Frank Duff would come to see him. Frank took this as a heavenly intervention and went to W. T. Cosgrave, head of Government, to ask him if he could get him an audience with the Holy Father since there was no hope of getting an introduction from the archbishop. Cosgrave took him to see the Nuncio and then made arrangements for his reception in Rome. Mr Cosgrave in fact gave the letter of introduction. Full of hope Frank started for Rome but up to the last moment it seemed doubtful whether the Pope would receive him. At last however it came to pass and Frank was allowed to present himself to Pius XI.

Already St Pius X had declared that it was more important to have a dozen apostolic laymen in each parish, than priestly vocations, Catholic schools or other institutions. Pius XI has passed into history as the Pope of Catholic Action. It was his heart's desire that the lay people in the Church should recognise their responsibility for evangelisation and respond to it. At his suggestion branches of Catholic Action were formed in many countries, mostly grouped according to sex or profession; Italy and France excelled especially in this regard. But unfortunately this movement tended more and more in later years to undertake a purely social apostolate, and finally in places it turned to politics. The conviction grew in its members that people were first to be offered favourable conditions of life, cultural and educational incentives, before one could talk to them about the faith. Frank fought this idea with the whole weight of his personality and had to suffer for it.

Frank went to Pius XI with Monsignor O'Brien of Liverpool. They had to submit a memorandum (translated into Italian). The Pope plied them with question after question, and then asked what they wanted of him. They were ready. Monsignor O'Brien speaking in French said: 'Holy Father, that you would say for our propaganda purposes that it was your wish to see the Legion extend all over the world.' There was a long pause and then the Pope replied, 'With all my heart I extend that wish.' Finally he got up, went towards Frank and embraced him. 'This thing is from God,' he said in a tone that betrayed his emotion. He had understood that this new movement corresponded to the idea he himself had formed about the task of lay people in the Church and had described in his Encyclical on Catholic Action. Contrary to numerous critics he liked the name 'Legion of Mary' and found it most suitable. Not long afterwards Frank received a letter from the Holy Father in which he granted a special blessing to the Legion of Mary, calling it a 'beautiful and holy work'. Rome had spoken.

15. The First Envoys

In the year 1932 the International Eucharistic Congress took place in Dublin. Visitors from numerous countries arrived in the Irish capital, among them a priest and a young woman from Australia. Both were enthusiastic about the Legion, and before the year ended the first praesidium was set up in Melbourne.

In South Africa the idea of the Legion became known through a young girl who, during a holiday in Ireland, had taken part in a pilgrimage to Lough Derg and had learned of the Legion there. Shortly afterwards there was a beginning in the Caribbean islands: Puerto Rico, Trinidad, Grenada.

In the year 1933 an Irish writer published an article on the Morning Star hostel and its inmates in an American periodical. Not long afterwards Frank received a letter from a certain Mr Oliver, a businessman in San Francisco. For years he had harboured the idea of a hostel for down-and-out men and believed it to be an urgent necessity in his home town. He asked that an experienced person be sent to the United States who could help to found such a hostel, and he would defray the expenses. Frank replied that the building and running of such hostels was not the only purpose of the Legion, not even its first aim, and then described the movement and its activity. Mr Oliver was all the more interested and renewed his request for an experienced adviser and then it could be seen whether the Legion of Mary was suitable for America.

A zealous young legionary who had already proved herself at the time of the Bentley Place affair agreed to take unpaid leave from her job for three months. The trip was originally meant only to explore the possibilities, but the success went far beyond all expectations. Several praesidia were started and the ground laid for others. Mr Oliver was enthusiastic and offered to finance the work of a legionary for three years. A volunteer was found and worked with outstanding success.

The work load in America was so great that the envoy's endeavours were not sufficient. Mr Oliver then decided to invite over two more representatives of the Legion. Whilst the first envoy returned home to Ireland after three years, the two others – a girl and a man – remained in America for twelve years. This was due partly to the outbreak of the Second World War which made the crossing of the Atlantic hazardous, but partly to the fact that the field of work was so vast. New possibilities appeared constantly and calls for help to start praesidia came frequently. It was a special characteristic of the Legion that it was able to gather black and white citizens around the same table – at the time a completely new and revolutionary idea. The legionaries found their way into neighbouring Canada where the idea of the lay apostolate was carried to the farthest Indian missions, and members sent greetings to the 'big white chief' in far away Ireland – a new title for Frank. These representatives of the Legion in foreign countries were called Legion envoys.

Frank loved his envoys with a truly fatherly affection. Correspondence with them, which in the beginning he managed alone, was an added burden, but also a much loved one. He knew how to counsel them in their doubts and to console them in their many difficulties and disappointments. He had already itemised in a special chapter of the *Handbook* the most frequent objections against the Legion and had answered them; but from different countries or continents new ones were constantly being expressed. The first one frequently being 'what is possible in Ireland cannot be done in this country'. It would be a difficult task to evaluate the thousands of letters which Frank Duff wrote to his envoys – a great pity, because these letters contain real jewels of wisdom and experience which would give comfort and strength to many, not only legionaries of Mary.

In 1933 Frank succeeded at last in giving up his position in the Department of Finance in order to devote himself solely to the Legion of Mary. This sounds as if there had been a diminution in his work load, but with the ever-faster growth of the Legion in all countries and continents, and with the growing number of Legion envoys, every minute of his time was taken up. However, it was a relief to be free of his professional duties and to be able to devote his immense energy to the work dearest to his heart – '. . . a step I was never in the remotest degree sorry for,' he avowed many years later.

Although Frank saw everything in a supernatural light he always kept both feet on the ground. A man of infectious optimism, he had no illusions about human weakness. One of his favourite sayings was: 'Nothing is as good and nothing as bad as we believe it to be'. If his envoys started to enthuse in the face of success, he warned them of disappointments, but if they were depressed he always knew how to comfort them from the treasury of his experience. I cannot resist the temptation to give here a small example of his advice to an envoy because it reflects his point of view so well: 'Let me once again proceed to exhort you to the securing of sleep. Don't regard time in bed as time taken from your mission. It is just the very opposite. . . Actually you are engaged in a battle, the whole result of which depends not upon your piety and not upon your activity, nor upon your powers of organisation, or your sense of conviction of the Legion. What is going to dictate the issue of the whole contest is stout nerves. If you lose your nerve you have lost the battle. . . so for heaven's sake cultivate that nervous system of yours far more jealously and more anxiously than the violinist would care for his Stradivarius'.

16. By their Fruits

St Teresa of Avila describes in the *Interior Castle* how a saintly person who has brought much fruit in the supernatural life, will very soon find companions to help him relish them. Frank Duff is an example. From the beginning he was followed by persons who in the Legion found a spiritual climate in which they could expand and develop. In one of the interviews recorded on video tape the interviewer, Al Norrell, asked Frank what he thought of the Legion as a maker of saints. Frank found this designation absolutely justified. 'The Legion of Mary,' he said, 'puts into the legionary mind the capacity for understanding the great Catholic doctrines: the doctrine of the Mystical Body, the Motherhood of Our Lady, the extraordinary influence of Our Lady with the Holy Spirit. These things are holy and sanctifying,' he added, 'and they make saints by the bushel.'

But one thing must not be forgotten: as Frank Duff declares in the *Handbook,* it would be completely wrong to consider mere membership in the Legion as a kind of holiness; it represents only the normal Catholic life. Seen from God's side, the saint is the normal person. About all others one can say what the German poet Hebbel so poignantly wrote about himself: 'the man I am, mournfully salutes the one I could have been.' It would be well worth while to describe in a collection of short biographies a few of these wonderful people who, first in Ireland but very soon on all continents, found a real mission in the Legion and knew how to respond to it. Here we must be brief, but a biography of Frank Duff would be incomplete without the mention of a few persons who were particularly dear to him, and whom he helped to discover and develop.

In order to have his spiritual sons and daughters always present in his thoughts and to keep their images before him he had a photograph taken of each. These photographs were framed and now hang in the Legion office. At first there were only four or five. Today the 'envoys gallery' as Frank affectionately called it, covers two entire walls of a large room. To his visitors from all over the world Frank would display the photographs with fatherly pride for these were his spiritual children.

One day Frank heard about a young girl who for some time belonged to the Legion and was considered as promising. The name of the girl was Edel Mary Quinn. He invited her to his home and spent an evening chatting with her. From that visit on he knew he was dealing with a unique personality. It is an interesting fact that the girl friend, through whom Edel had come into the Legion, had at first advised her not to join. Such a pretty, cheerful creature, she thought, would find little relish in the humdrum and often disappointing spade work of the Legion. But Frank was a good judge of human nature. When one of the praesidia involved with the derelicts needed a new president he decided that Edel should take over the office. She was only twenty years old at the time. There were strong protests from members; what was needed was an experienced mature person and they were sent a child! But Frank said: 'Wait and see' and soon the members of the branch knew that they were fortunate in their new president.

Edel intended to join the Poor Clares later on but had to give up this plan when she developed tuberculosis. After a year and a half in a sanatorium she returned to her secretarial work and to her Legion involvement, better but not cured.

Many Irish legionaries at the time went to England

during their holidays and travelled mostly on bicycles, since cars were not yet very plentiful, from parish to parish in an effort to enthuse priests and lay people for the Legion which they themselves loved so much. Edel took part in one of these trips and contrary to all expectations, endured the physical hardships very well. She then planned to move over to England altogether in order to devote herself to the extension of the Legion among the Irish communities. But the central council of the Legion received a letter from a bishop in Africa who had come to know the Legion during a holiday in his native Ireland. He asked that a representative be sent to work in East Africa. Frank thought at once of Edel and she was extremely happy about the offer.

The thought of sending this delicate girl to the African mission caused a storm of indignation, but Edel knew her life would probably be short and it seemed desirable to her to devote the years that were left to the service of God, and Frank understood and supported her. To this day some people think that his decision was not right.

If Frank had listened to the warning voices and kept Edel in Ireland, she would have been one of those hundreds of Legion sisters who faithfully fulfilled their weekly task until the Lord puts an end to their activity. But by supporting her in her desire to go to Africa, Frank opened new possibilities of evangelisation on an entire continent, and for Edel herself the way to heroic sanctity. During the eight years of her work she accomplished wonders. When she finally reached the end of her life she had already become a legend. Twelve years after her death the process for her beatification was started and is proceeding very well. From the boat which took her to Africa she wrote a letter to Frank which shows how she felt herself to be understood by him. 'It is good to be trusted,' she wrote, 'that will help in the days to come. . . I am glad you let me go. The others will be glad later.'

'The others will be glad later'. . . these were prophetic words. Edel would not have allowed any other person such a profound insight into her soul. 'She was the <u>total product of the Legion of M</u>ary,' Frank said once about her – 'its <u>quintessence,</u> so to speak.'

But he who created and offered to her the framework for her saintly life was – under God – Frank Duff.

17. Far and Near

An observer once declared that at Legion headquarters people were better informed about religious conditions in the world than the officials in the Vatican, because in Dublin they received completely untrimmed reports. This knowledge was stored in Frank Duff's phenomenal memory. He was conscious of this wonderful gift. If that memory in the course of time grew to even wider dimensions, it nevertheless affectionately retained the remembrance of friends and helpers from his youth and from early times of the Legion, of small happenings – especially those with a humorous side – or of special habits and funny sayings of old acquaintances. He loved to recount these stories and could always heartily laugh about them. Several of his friends and fellow legionaries of those times also possessed a good sense of humour, Jack Nagle and Jimmy Cummins, both of whom have since gone to their reward, were among them. Jimmy was an excellent mimic. This resulted in many a side-splitting evening which none of those present will ever forget. Frank loved to tell jokes; his memory helped him in this respect so that he had a wealth of them in store and he usually laughed heartily while recounting them. Some of the Legion sisters around him found this side of his nature not quite fitting for the saintly man they considered him to be. They liked to ask the foreign visitors what they thought of Mr Duff. If the reply was as expected: 'A wonderful man,' they would add half excusingly: 'Well, he has just that little weakness. He likes to tell jokes. . .' It is strange that while in the Legion of Mary the members call each other 'Brother' and 'Sister', they always spoke of Frank as 'Mr Duff'.

Frank had the gift of never letting his people feel he was pressed for time. His obligations might be most urgent but anyone talking to him had the impression that Frank had unlimited time for him; time and interest. He was entirely at the disposal of each person. Each one felt himself to be understood and taken seriously. His love and understanding belonged especially to the poor and derelict.

'Till the Legion in any centre can say with truth that its members know personally, and are in touch in some way with each and every individual member of the degraded classes, its work must be regarded as being still in a state of incomplete development, and efforts in this direction must be intensified,' he had written in the *Handbook*. Throughout his life he tried to fulfil this requirement, but his heart-warming goodness and kindness did not come from weakness. If one of the inmates of Regina Coeli came home drunk and kicked up a row — a not infrequent happening — Mr Duff was called in. He always knew how to bring her to her senses, if needs be by main force, and he was physically very strong.

He loved children, and they loved him. Walking from his home to the Legion office, he was very often surrounded by a crowd of children, mostly the offspring of the unmarried mothers in the hostel. Each one wanted to be taken up or caressed by him. If legionaries brought their children to him, friendship was immediately established. No child was shy in front of him.

When Frank Duff spoke about the subject he had most at heart, the apostolate, he was seized by a fire which became almost physically perceptible. He knew how to enthuse his listeners in such a manner that they themselves began to glow. They left him with the feeling that now they were ready to go to the ends of the earth and to accept everything, including martyrdom. Once when a legionary who was setting out on a mission mentioned this fact to him he replied with a smile: 'You have to be properly warmed up because you will have a hard nut to crack.'

What struck people particularly about Frank was his profound personal humility and modesty, whilst at the same time being utterly convinced of the Legion's importance to the Church. He would never have dreamt of taking credit for the wonderful extension of the Legion, or to claim for himself the merits of its achievements. In his correspondence he mainly used the 'pluralis modestatis'. He nearly always spoke about 'us' if he had something personal to report. The word 'I' appeared very seldom in his letters. On the other hand he had the courage, especially in later years, to call the Legion 'the right arm of the Church'. The fact that apostolic work was so forgotten, so neglected in the everyday life of Catholics, hurt him like an open wound that never healed. He believed that a non-apostolic Christianity must lead to complete loss of faith within two generations. Witness to this are many of his letters in which he again and again returned to this subject. 'What a. . . type of teaching which has been the common doctrine of the Church in these later times! Practising Catholicism was taught as a sort of perfection. The idea of apostleship was never taught; in many quarters it was expressly denied to the laity. And they expect such a Catholicism to stand up to Russia.' (16 October 1946)

'You mention a common difficulty voiced by the priests whom you have interested in the general subject of the Legion: "We have no one of the necessary standard here." Oh, but that is a mistake, and likewise it represents the product of a grave fault on their part. They thereby admit that never before have they attempted to put such standards before the laity, which means that they have never proposed to them the idea of an apostolate at all. . . Let parents try the experiment of always keeping a baby in bed, never permitting it to use its little legs, never presuming that it is to be called upon to do any more than lie helplessly there. . . well, that is what the priests in general have been doing with the lay people. They start bemoaning things when the said lay people will not lift a finger for religion, will not be true to it, will betray it when the occasion arises, will massacre the priests when thoroughly annoyed with them.' (17 May 1947)

And a last example: 'It is true that "the serpent has to exhibit himself before he can have his head crushed by Our Lady. I would urge a converse to that saying, i.e. that likewise Our Lady must go after the serpent if the aim be to crush it. . . but she cannot do so except through human agencies, and this is where the modern apostolic idea seems to break down altogether. Our Lord and Our Lady have to do all the apostleship themselves. We pray to them to do it, and the supposition is that then it operates. But this is not the Christian idea at all. Our Lord and His Mother can only operate through those human agencies which must present themselves – and that not in any passive sort of way, waiting to be moved and deployed. The said agencies have to be positive and active on their own account, and only to the extent that they are, will Our Lady enter into them and avail of them as instruments of her maternity of souls."' (1 April 1950)

18. Into the Whole World

A legionary with literary ability refused to write a biography of Frank Duff because she thought that such a work would just become a history of the Legion of Mary. She was right. The life of Frank Duff cannot be separated from the Legion. It is his life; all else was peripheral. This biography is in no way destined for legionaries of Mary only, even though they may be the first to interest themselves in it. But a man like Frank Duff belongs to the whole world, not to a single movement. We hope that many people, who know nothing about the Legion of Mary, will read this book. It is important to show and explain to them the work of Frank Duff.

Before the outbreak of the Second World War the Legion had spread to the five continents but its presence had been most remarkable in the English-speaking countries. The few trips to other countries which Frank undertook did not always have an immediate success.

The first non-Irish envoy to make her appearance was Maria Diepen from the Netherlands. She began legionary work in her native country and only in later years continued this work abroad in the Guianas and the Dutch West Indies. A Dutch priest had translated the *Handbook* into his native language and this proved very useful. Ireland's neutrality during the war made it possible for Frank to keep in touch with Legion branches all over the world. Very encouraging reports were coming from England. In spite of the war conditions and the blitzkrieg the praesidia met regularly and the members fulfilled their apostolic tasks as if circumstances were normal. Some of the branches transferred their meetings from weekday evenings to Sunday mornings because movement during the blackout was difficult and at times dangerous, especially for Legion sisters, and the air raids took place mostly at night. In the periodical *Maria Legionis* which had been started shortly before the outbreak of the war and which appears every three months, there is an amusing report from 1942. Two members of a praesidium were making their Legion promise, but after almost every paragraph the whole group had to dive under the table for protection from bombs. Meetings were held at times in air raid shelters and the members said the Rosary aloud in the shelters and they invited those present to join in. Even juniors, members under eighteen, showed undaunted courage and determination.

Similar reports came from Malta where despite ceaseless air raids the Italian and German bombers did not succeed in conquering the island or even discouraging its population. After the end of the war, the British royal family conferred the George Cross for outstanding bravery on the island as a whole. The Maltese Legion of Mary remained intact in spite of the raids and continued its work in face of danger.

A start was made in France in the midst of the war – something Dublin had not expected. This was the work of a young Irish girl, Veronica O'Brien, who had refused to return home despite grave warnings. 'I shall return when I have started the Legion here,' she wrote from Paris, 'not sooner'. That was the last news received from her for some time. When the German army, which at first had occupied the north of the country, moved southwards, Veronica joined the stream of refugees in flight from the approaching troops. They were constantly exposed to attacks from low-flying German aircraft; frequently they had to take cover. Hungry and pale with no belongings other than the clothes she was wearing, Veronica finally arrived in Nevers. Here she found hospitality in the convent of St Gildard, the convent of Saint Bernadette Soubirous. There she helped with the distribution of hot soup to the exhausted and shivering refugees. The next news from her that reached Dublin reported the start of seven praesidia.

Even in the midst of hostilities no frontier seemed closed to the Legion. On German soil the first praesidium with eighteen members was set up in the camp 'Stalag 383' for prisoners of war. An Australian soldier carried the *Handbook* in his pocket even when he went into action and he found it easy to enthuse his fellow prisoners for the idea. While this branch was naturally disbanded at the end of the war, another one set up by French forced labourers has survived to this day.

In Italy, after the landing of the Allied Forces near Anzio and Nettuno, a praesidium was set up by a unit of British soldiers. They carried it north as they advanced through the peninsula. In Rome they were received by Pope Pius XII who had heard about these stalwarts and wished to meet them. When he asked them whether they had any request to make to him they asked for permission to start the Legion in Rome. They were convinced that the population urgently needed such a movement. After the war there were opportunities to introduce the Legion to many other countries. In Dublin the members were praying for envoys suited to the task. Frank found them at the right moment. For Germany, a legionary from Vienna offered herself; she had been a refugee in England during the war and had learned about the Legion there. An Irish girl fluent in Italian went to Italy. Two remarkable Filipino girls came forward: Joaquina Lucas, lecturer at Manila University, left her position and went to South America. She was to work for the Legion for twenty years in different countries. Pacita Santos, a young lawyer from Manila, left her clients and her family not long afterwards and went as an envoy to Spain where up to that time the Legion had not been introduced. Spanish missionaries had long ago brought the Catholic faith to the Philippines and Pacita was happy to be a missionary to their country. A Chinese girl, Teresa Su, went to Indonesia. Many other countries welcomed Legion envoys. A young man from eastern Europe had come to Ireland as a refugee and joined the Legion there; he had then entered the Dominican order but he left with the agreement of his superiors who thought that the introduction of the Legion to his native country was more important than remaining in the monastery. He went back, lived through many adventures – at one time even landed in prison; but he succeeded in making the Legion known in his homeland. A similar case is that of a young man whom Frank never met in person. A young man from the Volga district in the Soviet Union had come to Germany as a prisoner of war. After the war he decided to settle there. When the Legion was established in his parish in Moenchengladbach he became president and soon proved his apostolic worth. After some time he declared to his parish priest that he considered it his duty to extend the Legion to Soviet Russia and he wanted to apply for repatriation.

The parish priest was impressed but warned: 'Don't you know what happens to those repatriated?'

'I do know. They are sent to Siberia for five years to be re-educated. But I am young and strong; I can wait for five years. So I shall either suffer martyrdom or start the Legion. And when you hear from me, even though it be only a picture postcard, you will know that I have reached my objective.'

For almost six years the priest heard nothing and often wondered whether the young man was still alive. Then a picture postcard arrived from a camp in Siberia, and later the priest got several letters which in coded form told about his work. Frank took the liveliest interest in this case which he was informed of by a correspondent. He had the Soviet Union particularly at heart and followed up with the greatest interest every opportunity which presented itself in this area. He ended one of his letters in this way: 'We must get into Russia. WE MUST GET INTO RUSSIA.'

With all the fatherly tenderness which Frank felt for his legionaries, and especially the envoys, he nevertheless expected unconditional dedication from them. He had the courage to call for heroism. One of his envoys had to undergo a major operation. This hit her so hard, physically and mentally, that she was thinking of returning home. Frank wrote to another one of his spiritual daughters who shortly before had got over similar trouble: 'Referring to P., you remark that the proper advice to give her is that she should resolutely hold on. That is definitely what I would wish to have said to her, but unfortunately it is one of those things that cannot be said. Your position would appear to have been worse than hers and yet you fought through it all on your feet. . . It seems to me that these occasions form the providential testing point for a mighty mission of the Envoy type. If the future of a country is going to be changed it is not by parlour methods. . . but by sweat and blood. Every now and then the test is applied to one. The mission is put in one scale and one's own advantage is put in the other. If one chooses the latter, the great game has been lost. I think that one has to be so resolute on one's mission that if the alternatives present themselves: the mission or my life, one has to choose the mission.' (12 May 1949)

19. Big Crosses, Small Crosses – But always the Cross

The tasks that kept Frank on the move day after day never interfered with his affection for his family. He was particularly attached to his mother but also had a close relationship with his brother and sisters. With the exception of his mother who was physically and mentally strong to the end, none of his relatives seemed to possess Frank's stamina. Within a few years he lost one member after another of his immediate family circle. The first was his sister Isabel who died in June 1949. To a letter of sympathy he replied: 'I am more than grateful for your kind sympathy in regard to my loss. I must say that people have been extraordinarily good, and unquestionably a mighty volume of prayer has proceeded upwards for the repose of my sister's soul. People do not appreciate the amount of consolation that is derived from such things by the relatives of the departed one.' At the same time his brother's health declined. On several occasions he had to go to hospital but he always seemed to recover. However, in the end there remained little hope. 'My brother continues very ill,' Frank wrote in the month of August 1949, 'and does not seem to be improving. . . My own verdict concerning him is that they have succeeded in poisoning him with the innumerable remedies and injections that they have been pouring into him.' John died on 20 August 1949, only two months after Isabel.

The worst blow was still to come: the sudden death of his mother at the beginning of 1950. Frank was terribly shaken. 'The blow has been an awful one, the worst one of my life. Adding it on to the disasters which preceded it, I do not know where I really stand. It will take me some little time to settle down again and get my balance.' Such tones are rare in Frank's letters; he spoke this way only to his closest friends. He always remembered his mother with affection and grateful love. Long afterwards he replied to a friend of his who complained about the sufferings of ageing: 'You remark that getting old is a hard thing. No, I would not say that; it all depends. It is possible to grow old gracefully; my own dear mother did so. She retained the fullness of her faculties to the very end and quite a useful amount of bodily vigour, enough to make her circulate through town every day doing her shopping. She read a great deal and kept interested in everything. And through it all she was kind and sweet and always strong. How typical it was of her that when she got her big heart attack at five o'clock in the morning of 24 February and was in agony she contented herself with struggling to a chair and fighting through it. She said that she would not dream of wakening up any one of us! She certainly departed in the very manner that she would herself have wished – and probably that I too would wish in spite of the dire hurt of losing her. There was no twilight in her life, no period of mental decline and painful infirmity.'

Next there followed sorrow, not about a relative, but a friend whose loss shook Frank profoundly. Since 1948 Father Creedon had been ailing. He was the ever-faithful friend who had been Spiritual Director of the Concilium Legionis, the Central Council of the Legion, for more than a quarter of a century. Again and again there appeared to be a slight improvement but in the summer of 1950 it became clear that the end could not be staved off. During the last two nights Frank kept vigil at the dying priest's bed. Fr Creedon died on 29 July 1950. One year later Frank lost his young sister Ailis. She had contracted T.B. many years before and finally underwent an operation, but the hoped-for cure did not materialise. Frank's remaining sister Sarah Geraldine, herself a medical doctor was married to a doctor. She lived in Navan. Her house with a garden attached was always open to Frank. When he had urgent literary work to do he would go there because he was certain not to be disturbed.

Only very gradually did Frank get accustomed to life without his mother. He now took his meals in the Regina Coeli hostel where the two indoor sisters, Peggy McDonnell and Nellie Jessop cared for him with great love. Nellie had belonged to the Legion since 1932, when after the death of her husband she decided to devote her life to the service of the hostel. With her affectionate care and motherly understanding she succeeded gradually in giving Frank a feeling of home. Especially in later years she was a real support to him, though at times she did nothing but sit quietly beside him and comfort him with her presence.

Frank suffered almost unbearably through the loss of his family, particularly his mother, and there was hardly a day which did not bring him sad news from some quarter with regard to the Legion of Mary. His envoys were accustomed to regarding him as their 'wailing wall'. They would always unload on him the many difficulties and disappointments which they encountered in the course of their work. If at times they felt remorse of conscience on this account, he would comfort them by declaring that he was really there to encourage and help them, and that he liked doing it. That was certainly true, but what a burden it was! If things were going well in one country, bad news would without fail arrive from another. Nothing was so improbable, nothing so odd that it did not happen at one time or another. A legionary in Italy discovered that a movement had been started by an Italian priest, calling itself the Legion of Mary. The priest had already applied to various bishops for sanction of his movement. To the objection that a Legion of Mary was already in existence he declared simply that this was an Irish Legion which did not concern him. His organisation disappeared long ago without leaving a trace. Another organisation of the same kind exists to this day: a small but resolute African sect calls itself 'Legion of Mary' and as such, has caused a lot of confusion.

An Italian priest who had fostered the introduction of the Legion in his area unfortunately went off the rails and – together with a few young girls, who originally had formed a praesidium, rebelled against his ecclesiastical superiors. Since admonition was of no avail, he was finally suspended and his followers excommunicated. Although only about a dozen people were involved the next day Italian newspapers carried headlines saying that the Legion of Mary had been excommunicated and from now onward was forbidden in Italy.

In France a powerful bishop antagonistic to the Legion had a member of a religious order which opposed the Legion compose a pamphlet of the worst kind in which every feature of the movement was disparaged and ridiculed. 'Absolute hell is let loose in France against the Legion,' Frank wrote. 'Probably the cause of it is the fact that the Legion has now extended into thirty-eight of the dioceses, so that the possession of one or two more would give it an actual majority. The contemplation of this swing-over has upset official Catholic Action greatly. They have enlisted the services of a prominent priest to write a long alleged analysis of the Legion. To apply the word analysis to so unworthy a document is to libel the word "analysis". . . This document has been circulated through France with an assiduity and fervour worthy of a better cause. In a trice it has appeared in the hands of nearly every priest. As a result a regular wave of hatred against the Legion has been started moving. . . Some bishops who had given permission to start have withdrawn it, and others are stated to be wavering and inclined to withdraw sanctions already given. The legionaries themselves are reduced to a state of regular terror and dismay. It is even said that an appeal is to be made to Rome to declare the Legion inopportune for France. . . If one-tenth of this false zeal had been shown for the interests of religion instead of against true religion things would be better in France today. Of course in reality there is nothing to be feared. This is purely a devil's storm, and such storms are fierce but do not last long. Then when they pass everybody is left wondering what it had all been about. There is one good thing in it all however. It is that the Legion has been given a degree of advertisement which money could not have secured for it.'

Not a day passed without some disastrous news from some quarter. From these experiences Frank had formed his concept of the 'devil's storm' because, strangely enough, these events followed the same pattern nearly everywhere. An attack seemed about to wipe out the Legion in a particular country to the dismay of the legionaries – then suddenly things continued as if nothing had happened. Frequently there was new growth afterwards. However, these 'devil's storms' did not leave Frank unmoved; he sympathised too strongly with the difficulties of his spiritual children to be indifferent. One envoy was struggling with failing health. To her Frank wrote: 'It is deplorable that the immense labours of your. . . occupation should be added to by this disability, but I suppose that the whole thing is mystical in its character, i.e. you have to be loaded up to the last notch. It is according to your determination, which is only tested by the amount you are bearing, that it will be given to you in the way of conquests. In the day that you are able to bear upon your shoulders the whole woe of xxx, in that day you have gained all xxx.' If Frank could write that, it was because he had himself tasted these things to the dregs.

In another letter he was even more outspoken: 'You remark that you know that I do not take your depressions seriously at all. Therein you are wrong. I take them very seriously, for I regard them as menacing your entire envoyship. Depression hopelessly biases your judgment. No judgment that you would form and utter in such a time would possess the slightest value... Depression gives the effect of exhausted physical resources. That effect operates very much the same as if the resources were really gone. One is not able to do things. The burden which, in absolute reality, is well within our capacity crushes us to the ground. I know all this because I have been through every possible shade and variation of the thing.' Crosses from without, crosses from within, big crosses, small crosses – Frank always stood firm like a rock. Few people suspected how much it cost him.

20. Baptism of Fire in China

In the meantime, in a country which seemed to justify the highest hopes, a 'devil's storm' was brewing which was to last more than thirty years. As a young secretary at the Dublin Nunciature, Antonio Riberi had come to know Frank and the Legion. Years later he was made an archbishop and appointed Nuncio to East Africa where he met Edel Quinn. He had supported her in every possible way, had written to all the bishops of his territory recommending the Legion of Mary to them. His enthusiasm for the movement still grew when he observed the wonderful success of Edel's work. 'The Legion of Mary is a miracle of these modern times,' he had declared.

After the Second World War Archbishop Riberi was transferred to China as Internuncio. Here too he had immediately written to the bishops and advised them to start the Legion – this in view of a possible victory of the communists who had already started their 'long march' from the north. He entrusted the extension of the Legion of Mary to the Irish Columban Father Aedan McGrath. Up to now the Legion had not made much headway in China although there were praesidia in Peking. Things changed dramatically. What happened was unique in the history of the Legion. The young generation, particularly the students, thronged into the movement. A German priest who was a professor at the Fu-Jen University in Peking told us that one morning a group of young people had approached him, asking him to start a praesidium and take over its spiritual direction. In the afternoon of the same day another group came to see him. They too wanted to set up a praesidium. Before the end of the week the Father had as many as he could cope with. This expansion was in no way limited to Peking; it covered the whole country.

Simultaneously there was a tremendous upsurge of conversions, again mostly among the young generation. Archbishop Riberi was overwhelmed. He saw his highest hopes confirmed and reported to Rome that the country could expect conversions on a great scale. In Dublin enthusiasm was not so strong. Frank had always considered the quality of legionaries as more important than numerical strength. He was afraid of a mushroom growth which might water down the spirit and performance of the members. Both were in fact mistaken. The Chinese legionaries soon proved their worth and their loyalty to the Legion, but Archbishop Riberi's optimism received a damper. Mao-tse-tung over-ran the country with his communist hordes. Within a few years the whole country was conquered and the leader of the Chinese nationalists, Chiang-kai-Chek went into exile in Taiwan.

At first the communists tried to win the legionaries to their side and to use them for the setting up of a 'national church', but this plan failed and the opposite occurred. Wherever the Legion existed the setting up

of the national church was unsuccessful because the legionaries did excellent educational work among the Catholic population, warning them against separation from Rome.

It soon came to an open struggle between the state and the Legion. It had to drop its public activities and could only hold its meetings in secret. At the beginning of 1952 it was officially declared to be a reactionary organisation and forbidden throughout China. The members had to present themselves to the police in order to be registered. The officers were imprisoned, foremost among them Father Van Coillie, a Belgian priest who had been Spiritual Director of the Peking Senatus. Many priests who had been active in the Legion underwent 'special treatment'. They had to remain on their feet for days on end, were denied sleep, were subjected day and night to endless questioning and for months were fettered, feet and hands, with iron chains. What the communists were looking for with fanatic thoroughness were secret radio stations, weapons and espionage rings which would at last unveil the secret of the inexplicable impact of the Legion, but what they found were *Handbooks,* candles, statues of Our Lady. What they did not find in spite of endless searchings was that spirit which at the first Pentecost had gathered the apostles around Our Lady and inspired them to undertake valiant action.

The communists not only hated the Legion, they were afraid of it. Slander, organised baiting, brutal force – everything possible was employed to suppress the movement. The Legion was the 'public enemy No. 1'. Across all main roads in the big cities there hung banners on which it was publicised as a 'reactionary espionage organisation of the Vatican'. Many books have been written about the heroic resistance of the Chinese legionaries. The exact number of victims will probably never be known, but it is estimated that about two thousand legionaries were killed, whilst more than twenty thousand were thrown into prison. Those who were still free were subject to brainwashing. A document was drawn up in which the Legion was described as a secret fascist organisation with the sole purpose of maintaining the capitalistic society. Some members were called to the police two or three times every day; they had to learn by heart the wording of that document and were endlessly asked to repeat it. Some of them at last confessed something, in order to avoid the torture of continuous questioning. They were assured that they would not be punished if they presented themselves of their own free will and left the Legion, but many were imprisoned or shot regardless of what they did. The entire Catholic world was at that time looking on at the great drama taking place in China and stood full of admiration before the example of invincible faith shown by the legionaries. Pope Pius XII encouraged the Chinese Catholics in a special letter.

Fr McGrath spent three years in prison before being expelled from the country. He needed several years in Ireland to restore his impaired health and recover from the sufferings and tortures. Archbishop Riberi had been under house arrest for several months; he too was at last expelled. Immediately after his arrival in Hong Kong he sent Frank a telegram in which he expressed his conviction that the Legion would save the faith in China, even though the last priest or missionary might be imprisoned or killed. Was he right? We do not know as yet. But there are rumours to the effect that the number of Catholics in China has more than doubled during the thirty years of persecution.

Gobbet

21. . . . And Rome has spoken once more

In the autumn of the year 1952 Frank received a letter from the State Secretary in the Vatican conveying an invitation from the Pope to visit the Holy City. It was a great and happy surprise, all the more so as the obstacles which certain priests put in the way of the Legion still persisted. How different was this journey from the one on which Frank had ventured more than twenty years before as an unknown layman! John Murray who had worked for twelve years as Legion envoy to the United States and now was Vice-President of the Concilium, accompanied Frank. They stayed in the Irish Embassy to the Holy See. The ambassador at the time was Joe Walshe, who had been secretary of the Department of Foreign Affairs in Ireland for many years and was an old friend of Frank's. At the airport they were met by Archbishop Van Lierde OSA, the Sacristan of the Holy Father. They spent seventeen days in Rome, full to the brim with meetings and conferences. The climax was the private audience which Pope Pius XII granted them. 'I am very grateful to the Legion of Mary for the great services it has rendered to the Church,' the Holy Father declared, and Frank remarked that these words were spoken 'with indescribable warmth and love'. To all the legionaries in the world the Pope sent his special blessing. Frank had to give no fewer than thirteen conferences during this short time, mostly in colleges and seminaries. In the College of Propaganda Fide he spoke to four hundred students belonging to forty nations and all five continents. One hundred and fifty-five students attended his lecture in the North American college. Next he was invited to describe on Vatican radio the spirituality and history of the Legion. His address was broadcast in twenty-five different languages. The *Osservatore Romano* carried a report about the visit of the two legionaries. The generalates of various missionary orders were visited, and it became obvious that the Legion was considered an outstanding means of evangelisation in the countries of the Third World. Added to this were audiences with a number of cardinals, mainly those in charge of the various congregations of the Curia.

Special mention is due to Cardinal Tisserant, Dean of the College of Cardinals and Secretary of the Congregation for the Eastern Church. He had for some time shown a profound understanding of the intentions and possibilities of the Legion. He and Frank understood each other from the first moment, and he secured a permission for the Legion which is unique in the Church of God: that is permission to accept Orthodox Christians in its praesidia, that is, Christians who are not united to Rome, and also to start praesidia among the Orthodox communities. That happened more than ten years before the decree on Ecumenism of the Second Vatican Council! Unfortunately, the hopes which Frank attached to this permission have not materialised up to now. There have been tentative steps in this direction, and in Buenos Aires a praesidium of Orthodox emigrants from Russia was set up but it did not last. However, as Frank was to declare later, the Legion of Mary is only at the beginning of its activities. Probably this magnificent possibility will only have its full effect when the Legion of Mary succeeds in entering Russia on a large scale. Details for the setting up of praesidia within the Orthodox rite were fixed at that time. Instead of the statue of Our Lady which forms the centre of every Legion meeting, the praesidia of the Orthodox Christians were to use an icon of Mary, as statues are not customary in the Eastern Church, and instead of the Rosary which is unknown to the Orthodox, the members were to recite the *Hymnus Akathistos,* a litany which roughly corresponds to the length of the Rosary. The *Akathistos* was in the end found to be unsuitable and a form of prayer akin to the Rosary, but of Orthodox origin, was finally adopted. Frank however nourished the secret hope that with the Legion the Rosary would gain entrance into the Eastern Church. He often talked about it to his friends. Cardinal Tisserant too was hoping for a speedy extension of the Legion in the churches of the Eastern rite. He did not live to see the fulfilment of this hope.

The General Procurator of the Holy Ghost Fathers, Dr Murphy, wrote shortly after the Roman visit to an Irish friend: 'No potentate, no head of state has ever been received here with more genuine affection on the part of all the officials of the Church in Rome. . . and these audiences were not merely formal interviews. They were genuine expressions of affection and of gratitude to the Legion for the work it has done and is doing throughout the world. Mr Duff and Mr Murray are deeply moved by the intense conviction and warmth of the sentiments expressed.'

Before he left Rome Frank received a telegram from Monsignor Montini, then the Pope's under-secretary of State – later Pope Paul VI: 'Occasion your departure from Rome, Holy Father renews expression paternal affection, cordial interest in work of Legion of Mary, invokes continued divine assistance on organisation's praiseworthy activities, lovingly imparts to yourself, to officers and to legionaries throughout world SPECIAL apostolic benediction.' It was a great comfort. Frank needed it and was to need it in the future.

22. Sorrows and Joys

For some time it had become obvious that in the next edition of the Legion *Handbook* certain changes and additions would be necessary. This book, which in the beginning had appeared as a thin brochure, grew in the course of years to be a substantial volume of some four hundred pages as new works of the Legion, new aspects of its spirituality were included. With the exception of certain quotations from scripture or from theological works, mostly added at the end of each chapter, all the contributions came from Frank. For a long time he knew from experience that in Dublin he could not devote himself to any intense or continuous work. Visitors from many countries would succeed each other without leaving him a minute's respite and the burden of correspondence grew at times to be intolerable. 'I can only repeat,' he wrote to a friend who complained about his long silence, 'what I said regarding the delay: that I have seldom had such a difficult time. Things conspire against me in an astonishing manner. If I could count on getting a few hours every afternoon for my correspondence I would be able to cope with it. This does not seem an unreasonable requirement on my part, but nevertheless I am denied those few hours. If I get three afternoons in the week I am able to deem myself lucky. I am available every evening in the week for interviews from seven until eleven, but this does not satisfy people. You would imagine from their insistence that they get a day appointment, that the ordinary working hours were reversed and that people's free time was during the day!' Such sighs become ever more frequent in Frank's letters. In order to cope with the re-writing of the *Handbook* his only solution was to 'escape' to his sister in Navan. There he could work undisturbed. Of course he could not absent himself from the capital for any length of time because he would not then have been able to cope with the accumulated work. Accordingly, he always stayed in Navan for a week at a time. At last, after three or four visits to Navan the work was done – at least as far as it depended on Frank. What followed now one would like to cover with the cloak of Christian charity, but that would be an injustice to Frank because his life is to be described here, and that includes his trials.

The *Imprimatur* for the new edition of the *Handbook* was delayed on the flimsiest pretexts for years. At last it arrived – with the order to change some phrases in the *Handbook*. Since these were not really important, Frank was always willing to oblige. Then the game was repeated. After a further period of fruitless waiting came a new demand for more change. Since the Legion had already gained entrance into numerous countries, this delay had worldwide consequences. For instance the German edition of the *Handbook* was out of print; a reprint was imperative and a new translation seemed to be indicated. Naturally the legionaries waited for the appearance of the new book, but this did not come. Without the *Handbook* further expansion of the Legion became extremely difficult. A similar situation occurred with regard to the French *Handbook*. Frank was literally ground down between the urgent requests for the new *Handbook* and the delaying tactic of the ecclesiastical authorities. No wonder that one day he could stand it no longer and felt the overpowering urge to escape. He invited some of his friends who worked in the Morning Star to accompany him, and of course they were happy to do so. They jumped on their bicycles and off they went.

'We did a trip known as the Ring of Kerry,' Frank reported to a friend. 'We spent four days and a bit at it, covering 230 miles. To you. . . that seems a small figure, but it really represented big enough travelling, a great deal of it mountain climbing. We had one deplorable day which resulted in our being soaked clean through. The other days were lovely. We saw some utterly exquisite scenery. I came back feeling quite different in every way. Therefore the rather violent expedient has been a complete success.'

From now on Frank allowed himself a holiday once or twice every year and the effect was always the same – he would return refreshed and relaxed to the daily treadmill. He was more and more enthusiastic about the beauty of his native land which is easier to appreciate on a bicycle than from a car. In order not to have to keep this beauty solely in his memory he eventually started taking photographs. Thus began a hobby to which in later years he owed many a happy hour. He had a good eye for the proper angle and took pictures of artistic value. He liked to show his visitors the colour slides of his trips and, seeing them again, his joy was renewed. The daily performance of the cyclists was often amazing. At the age of sixty Frank was still able to cover sixty miles a day. The number of fellow-travellers grew from one year to the other and finally there was a permanent circle for which Frank invented the nickname of 'the Sprockets'. Very soon a young Passionist priest called Herman Nolan joined the group and so they now had a sort of private chaplain who received permission from the bishop to say Mass in any suitable room if there was no church within reach and so the problem of attending Mass was solved.

Frank returned from his first trip fortified to such an extent that he was again able to take up the question of the *Imprimatur* for the new *Handbook* and bear the waiting. Everything, be it good or bad, comes to an end, and at last the *Imprimatur* arrived and the book could be published.

The *Handbook* has been translated into more than sixty languages, and the number of copies distributed amounts to many millions, yet the publication of an edition never came smoothly. It was always obstructed by the most incredible difficulties and impediments. This might literally be a lesson for those who do not believe in the devil. Frank Duff did believe in him.

23. Alphonsus Lambe

Most chapters of this book refer necessarily to extended phases of activity so that it has been impossible to keep strictly in chronological sequence. Year after year brought its measure of sorrow and joy to Frank, each year so packed with events that it would suffice to fill the whole life of a less extraordinary human being.

In August 1954 Fr Toher was called to his reward. After Fr Creedon's death he had become Spiritual Director of the Concilium Legionis and for thirty-three years he had faithfully served the Legion of Mary; he had always been an understanding and sympathetic friend to Frank.

In the early nineteen fifties a very young legionary attracted attention. He had come to Dublin from the country. His name was Alphonsus Lambe, known to all as Alfie. Because of poor health he had to leave the Irish Christian Brothers and had found in the Legion of Mary a substitute for religious life. In his endeavours for the extension of the Legion in the rural districts of Ireland Alfie had shown great persuasive power and rare organising ability, and Frank had ventured to send him with an older colleague, as envoys to South America. What this young boy achieved there in five and a half years is legendary. He travelled all over the enormous continent by train, bus, plane, on horseback and on foot – Columbia, Ecuador, Peru, Bolivia, Brazil, Paraguay, Uruguay and Argentina were the scenes of his fruitful work. The difficulties he met in many places were a counterpart of the obstacles with which Frank Duff had to cope in Ireland. It is gripping to read how he gradually overcame them. And yet, this gigantic field of action did not suffice for his apostolic urge. He studied Russian and dreamed of going to the Soviet Union as Legion envoy. It was he who started a praesidium among the many Orthodox Christians who had come as refugees from Russia to Buenos Aires.

Frank followed the young man's activities with admiration and enthusiasm. It was a heavy blow to him when Alfie died from cancer in January 1959. He was only twenty-six years old. Alfie's grave has become the centre of many pilgrimages. The process of his beatification is in preparation.

'If the Legion of Mary had not done anything else than produce a man of the calibre of Alfie Lambe,' wrote Archbishop Tavella of Salta in a letter of condolence, 'it would already be a sign that it is blessed by God.' Most striking is the fact that after Alfie's death the movement to which he had devoted his whole strength grew very rapidly in the places where he had been working. Even in places where he met with the strongest resistance, as for instance in Buenos Aires, the Legion is thriving and growing. Many regions of South America have become centres and strongholds of the Legion of Mary. Frank Duff was allowed to witness this wonderful expansion. Once more, one of his spiritual children had given proof of the sanctifying force of the Legion's ideals, provided that one opens oneself unconditionally to its formative influence.

24. . . . And yet the Miraculous was there

We have seen that Frank was of the opinion that signs and miracles belong as naturally to Christ in his Mystical Body as they had formed an essential part of the life of Jesus. His faith was so unshakeable that he reckoned the Lord would perform a miracle if man had gone to the utmost limit of his forces without reaching his aim. 'He did not wait for miracles to happen, he just went and worked them himself,' declared Cardinal Ó Fiaich of Armagh in his obituary after Frank's death. Nevertheless Frank was a well-balanced person; his intellect ruling his will and sentiment. Fanaticism was alien to him, he had a wholesome dread of visions and ecstasies and, was downright proud of the fact that the Legion of Mary had come into being not only by a dispensation of Divine Providence, but due to human needs. Nevertheless his life was frequently accompanied by events which could be termed miraculous. These were not the most essential things in Frank's life; but if they were completely left out, something would be missing to round off the picture.

One day the Regina Coeli ran short of money. When asked what to do about it Frank replied: 'Make a novena to the Infant of Prague.' There was some shaking of heads behind his back; it would have appeared more reasonable to borrow money from a bank, but nobody liked to contradict Frank. Before the novena had come to an end an unknown lady appeared and handed in an envelope which contained a considerable sum of money – enough to meet the immediate needs. Perhaps this was just luck, but who is to say!

Another event was more extraordinary. Very late one night while Frank was as usual still working on his correspondence, the doorbell rang. In front of the house stood a dirty, ragged boy of about twelve. Frank could not get any satisfactory information from him except that he was lost and had nowhere to stay. He could not send him away so he gave him his own bed and slept on a couch downstairs. In the morning he went out to Mass. When he came in the domestic help had arrived. He was anxious that the presence of the unkempt youngster would not come to the notice of his family as they might not welcome the idea of vagrants staying in the house, so he said to the girl that there was a boy upstairs in his bed who was a bit dirty and uncared for. Could she look after him before the rest of the family were up and about. She said 'I don't know anything about any little tinker. When I came in a beautiful child came down the stairs, smiled at me and went out.' No doubt, it was the same boy. 'I believe that I welcomed the Lord Himself,' Frank said later on.

Something special occurred when Frank received a relic of the true Cross from a nun. It was not possible for us to get more details about the time of this gift, or the giver. It was only said that she had been convinced that the precious relic would be put to better use in Frank's hands than in her own. The relic had no authentication, and much as Frank tried to obtain one in the course of the years, he did not succeed. But he always carried the relic on his person and often declared that he did not really need an authentication – the miracles which this relic had worked were sufficient proof for him. Perhaps one day it will be possible for an investigator to describe all the miraculous happenings that were ascribed to this relic. According to Frank's own words, they were numerous. For instance, the sister of a priest friend of Frank's was to be operated on for a cancer of the breast. She asked Frank to bless her with the particle of the Cross. When she appeared at the hospital the cancer had vanished – to the amazement of the doctors. An American legionary took ill during a stay in Dublin; the diagnosis was ileus. He too was spared an operation after Frank blessed him with the relic. At times this force operated without Frank being conscious of it. When he was in Rome at the last session of the Council a mother with an epileptic son also visited the Holy City. The man got an epileptic fit after each Holy Communion. One day Frank was near him when it happened and put his hand over the man's forehead. In it he was holding the relic of the True Cross. Immediately the attack subsided. He never saw the man get another fit. After a while he noticed that mother and son used to eye him curiously, but they never actually spoke to him. As he was anxious that the favours accorded through the use of this relic would not be associated with himself, he always tried to get a priest to bless the person with it. In this case the occasion was too sudden for him to be able to think of the blessing.

Frank was rather wary of blessing with the relic. If the information about it had reached wider circles he would not have had a moment's peace. His friend of long standing, Canon Ripley of Liverpool who preached at the first Requiem Mass for Frank, referred to this fact. 'Already now,' he declared, 'many people ascribe miraculous things to him, but the greatest miracle is surely the Legion of Mary.'

I would like to conclude this chapter with a humorous episode: At a certain time, a woman lived in Dublin who developed a strange habit. She wrote numerous letters to priests and lay people who were active in the Legion or showed an interest in it. She informed them that Our Lady regularly appeared to her, letting her know all the things that were wrong in the Legion of Mary. Then there followed a whole catalogue of faults. At first Frank ignored this person, but when things got steadily worse Frank had 'quite a brainwave on the subject,' as he wrote. 'I sent her back through different quarters the statement that I had just had a revelation from the Blessed Virgin about her, and that part of the things revealed to me was that she was Stalin's cast-off wife. At once her written tirade ceased absolutely.'

25. New Flowers, New Sprouts

The development of the Legion in the mission countries was a steady one and for many years went on without particular climaxes or anticlimaxes. Towards the end of the nineteen fifties it seemed that in Europe also, where up to now it had met with great difficulties, there would be a faster growth.

Frank used to judge things in a very sober and realistic light. Frequently he had warned his envoys against exaggerated hopes if they enthused too much about certain persons or prospects. It was all the more striking then that he himself at that period showed an optimism which seemed to know no bounds. For instance, the number of praesidia in the Federal Republic of Germany had grown by one hundred in a single year. Frank believed quite seriously – and frequently stated his conviction in letters and conversations – that this number would shortly double. If finally the contrary was the case, it was due to circumstances to which we will return later on. But for the moment the tree which Frank had planted showed numerous and strong new shoots. First of all, the Patrician movement came into being. This consisted of discussion circles run by the Legion. They were to teach Catholics to rid themselves of their habitual shyness when asked to discuss religion. Although these circles are psychologically well planned and have stood the practical test very well, their diffusion met with great difficulties. This was probably due to the fact that especially after the Vatican Council, there were so many discussion groups that people soon had enough of them. They considered the Patricians to be another gathering where everything is subjected to questioning and made to look uncertain; and there is little positive result.

The *Peregrinatio pro Christo* developed very quickly and effectively being based on the medieval missionary journeys of the Irish monks. Here the legionaries devoted one or two weeks of their holidays to the apostolate. In groups they went to foreign countries where they either made visits from door to door or talked about the Catholic faith to people in the streets and squares, in the parks and public gardens. This idea spread and today not hundreds, but thousands of legionaries throughout the world go on missionary journeys every year. Mostly they return as changed persons. They are caught by a kind of fire so that they make light of sacrifices and exertions. There are legionaries who spend their holidays every year in this way. At a time when the parish missions are no longer held, many priests, in Great Britain especially, but also elsewhere, have recognised the value of having the entire parish visited door to door. Hence there are more and more petitions from priests to send them a team prepared to carry out this work. In the course of time this movement has widened in a twofold way. Those who for various reasons cannot take part in such a holiday apostolate, but do not want to forgo the experience, may go, generally in the company of their own praesidium, to a place nearby where they devote an entire day to evangelisation. On the other hand legionaries, especially young ones may give six months or a year to the Legion by going to a foreign country where they take on a job and devote all their free time to apostolic activity. This movement has given the legionaries the possibility of operating far beyond their own surroundings; it has saved countless praesidia from slipping into mere routine by engendering new enthusiasm. Frank's interest in this expansion was not only as a benevolent spectator; in many addresses and articles he instructed the participants about methods of approaching people. He pointed out the fact that for many persons to whom they talked in the streets or parks, this was the only chance in their whole life of being approached in the name of the Faith. Hence one had to avoid futile small talk and get at once to the essentials – the treasures which the Catholic Church holds for her children especially the Holy Eucharist and Mary, Mother of God and Mother of men. Finally he said every Catholic should be spurred to greater zeal and every non-Catholic invited to enter the Catholic Church.

Each year on the last week-end in October numerous 'peregrini' meet in Dublin to report about the experiences of the past year and plan new enterprises. Frank always insisted on giving to the participants, in his guiding addresses, the mental guidance for their future enterprises.

In the early nineteen sixties, shortly before the start of the Second Vatican Council, a priest who was Spiritual Director of the Legion of Mary in Italy devoted himself to the movement with particular enthusiasm. This was Monsignor Corrado Bafile. He had visited Dublin and made friends with Frank Duff. When Angelo Roncalli became Pope John XXIII he named Monsignor Bafile his Secret Chamberlain, but he left him complete freedom to continue working for the Legion of Mary. It was a great joy when Monsignor Bafile was named Apostolic Nuncio to the Federal Republic of Germany. Naturally, he invited Frank and other Concilium officers to attend his episcopal consecration. Frank hesitated for a long time to take upon himself the exertions of another trip to Rome because he found these trips abroad too strenuous. The Monsignor however insisted upon his presence, and since Frank did not wish to be discourteous he decided to make the trip. As he had done during former stays in the Holy City, he visited numerous dignitaries, especially Cardinals Agagianian and Tisserant, the superiors of various religious orders and the Legion in Rome which at that time had not yet gone beyond the status of a Curia.

More than 800 legionaries took part in Monsignor Bafile's consecration. They had come from all parts of Italy, and Monsignor, now Archbishop Bafile, gave a special reception for them after the consecration. The next day Pope John XXIII received the guests from Dublin in private audience. Archbishop Bafile accompanied and presented them to the Holy Father who had very complimentary things to say about the Legion. The news which reached Rome from all over the world, he said, proved its excellent system. Then he handed Frank a colour photograph of himself which he had signed. The text said that he conferred the apostolic benediction from his heart on all the legionaries in the world. The Pope underlined with his finger the words 'from his heart' and declared: 'These words are the truth; I have written them with my heart.'

Of all the generous praise which the Legion received from the popes in the course of the years, nothing went as far as Pope John XXIII's words on 15 July 1960 to a group of French legionaries – that the Legion of Mary was 'apt to show the true face of the Catholic Church to those who did not know it.'

26. Death Knocks at the Door

In spite of Frank's amazing physical strength he was not always in very good health, and suffered frequently from recurrent colds. Only to his closest friends would he confess how much he hated the cold. For the few steps from his house to the Legion office he never bothered to don a coat, not even in the depth of winter. He did not possess a hat, at any rate no one ever saw him with one, although in later years he wore a beret. At times he was unable for months to free himself from a head cold. Generally he did not heed it and just went on with his work. Only if there was absolutely no other way would he decide to stay indoors for a day or two. His deafness grew worse from year to year. He was very interested in technical progress in the field of hearing aids. Many legionaries will remember Frank using an unwieldy type of hearing aid box which looked like a transistor radio. He would place a small black box on the table and fasten to his ear a wire which came out from it. Later on he used the modern kind fitted behind the ear. When he heard about successful operations which had been performed on deaf people in London he decided to venture on such a step. At first it seemed to have been successful and after five days of absolute quiet the first sound reached his ear. It was for him a completely new experience to hear without artificial aid, but very soon his condition deteriorated once more. Another doctor in London declared after a thorough examination that he could restore Frank's hearing by further surgery. Frank had another operation but this time had the misfortune to catch an infection in the inner ear. Antibiotics and other medical remedies were administered to reduce infection, but Frank felt really miserable. Added to this was the fact that he never permitted himself a reasonable period of convalescence. As soon as he was a little better he threw himself once more into his frantic activity. There was no lasting cure for his deafness, even though at first his hearing seemed to be somewhat improved.

The only relaxation which helped Frank were his bicycle tours; he always returned fresh from them, but these excursions were never long enough to have a lasting effect. 'You are not here,' he wrote to a friend who had complained about his long silence, 'and you cannot possibly realise the sort of struggle I have been waging. This year has been the worst one in my history so far as failure to cope with things has been concerned. Only in the last few weeks have I managed to keep pace with my letters and even to go back and dig a little in the arrears. The contemplation of the resulting accumulation was unnerving; it represented a positive impossibility, once a letter had been passed over for a little while, to go back and look for it and then try to get one's thoughts into order for replying. So day by day the time slipped by. . .' Frank was at the time seventy-five-years-old, an age at which other people have already enjoyed for a long time, well-earned retirement. But for him, no such thing existed. He had been unwell for some time, but when he was asked to give a talk to the students of sociology at University College Dublin he accepted. When he entered the building he met the daughter of an old friend of his. She was training to be a nurse and knew Frank well. She was dismayed by his looks and advised him to call off his talk, but he refused. 'Think of it,' he admonished his listeners, 'that in your work you will never have to do with "cases". There are no cases, there are only human beings.' This saying might have almost been numbered among 'famous last words' because Frank collapsed as he had spoken them. He was taken to the Regina Coeli hostel. The young student nurse did the right thing: she telephoned Frank's sister and brother-in-law in Navan, who appeared at once and took the patient to their house where he got the attention he needed.

Frank did not know exactly what had happened to him, but he was prepared to die, and he did not mind it a bit. On the contrary, 'I was so happy at the thought of meeting my family again that I was almost disappointed when it did not materialise,' he confessed to a friend. 'I thought of dying,' he wrote a few days afterwards from his sickbed, 'but apparently it was only a case of complete exhaustion, so that something had to happen. It was not a stroke nor a heart attack.' It appeared later on after an x-ray that a blood vessel in the brain had burst, but the thrombus had clotted by itself and closed the vessel 'just as one mends a broken water pipe' according to Frank. He was lucky that he did not suffer from any serious after-effects such as paralysis or loss of speech. 'You really had a narrow escape' declared the specialist at the hospital in Dublin to which Frank had been taken because a bad gastric flu had developed. On Maundy Thursday Frank was anointed, but his strong constitution gained the day. After a convalescence of several months with his relatives in Navan he felt strong enough to return to Dublin. He looked much better and even had put on a little flesh. Naturally he was advised to take it easy and he promised to do so, but the only respite he allowed himself was a short siesta after lunch. It was not long before he resumed his full activity. The price in exhaustion and weakness which he had to pay for it had become even higher, but Frank paid it without hesitation.

27. Auditor at the Council

Even though Frank Duff had to fight resistance and hostility throughout his life he did not go short of personal recognition. The numerous awards and honours he received did not unduly impress him; he accepted them as something inevitable and forgot all about them immediately afterwards. The Holy Ghost Fathers and the De Montfort Fathers named him honorary member of their societies, which meant that he had a share in all their merits and good works. The congregation of the De Montfort Fathers also conferred on him their Marian Award.

From the University of Dayton, Ohio, he received the Marianist Award in 1956 for his distinguished work in Mariology. Frank went to the United States to accept it. At the same time he availed himself of the opportunity to visit several Legion councils and to give to them the encouragement and inspiration which the visitors had come to expect from him in Dublin. Pope John XXIII appointed him Knight Grand Officer of the Order of St Gregory, and the National University conferred on him the honorary Doctorate of Law, but he never put after his name the letters LL.D. to which he was entitled. The greatest honour was still to come.

When the Second Vatican Council started its sessions there were at first no lay auditors invited. Only gradually prominent Catholic philosophers and writers like Jean Guitton were called upon to take part in the sessions and later on the leaders of various lay organisations. To the amazement of various people Frank had not been invited at the beginning, but of course he could not have accepted then as he was still convalescing from his illness. 'You wonder why I have not been invited as a lay auditor to the Council,' Frank wrote to a friend. 'The fact has provided a fair amount of comment. Really I have no ideas on the subject. It has been quite impossible to diagnose the reasons which led to the inviting of those who were brought to Rome; some of them were really quite small fry indeed, and some of them, though prominent people, were not engaged in the ordinary apostolate. Here I would refer to such as Jean Guitton, the French writer. Then, the President of the Central Council of the St Vincent de Paul Society was not, so far as I am aware, invited. . . The question however is in the sentimental order only because, if I had been invited, I could not have gone. The health issue settled all that.'

Cardinal Suenens, the Archbishop of Malines in Belgium, was a great friend of the Legion. Years earlier he had written a theological commentary on the Legion

Promise, also a biography of Edel Quinn. He had said that it was he who pointed out to Pope Paul VI that Frank merited an invitation to attend the Council as a lay auditor and was invited to the last session.

Frank would not have been a normal human being if he had not been gratified by this honour. His state of health had sufficiently improved in the meantime, so that he could face the journey. The Irish Dominicans of San Clemente in Rome offered him hospitality, so he was in a familiar environment. Father Herman recounts that he met Frank on the day before his departure. He walked cheerfully to and fro in front of the Regina Coeli hostel and replied to the greeting of the priest: 'I have just decided to take a little part in the Council.'

On 11 September Frank boarded the special plane which took the Irish Bishops to Rome as well as some Scottish and English dignitaries. The flight lasted only three hours, and Frank remembered his first journey to Rome in 1931 which had taken two and a half days by train and boat.

For the legionaries of the Rome Senatus it was wonderful to have their founder amongst them. At the airport a delegation met him and took him to his living quarters. The day after his arrival, a Sunday, they showed him some of the sights of Rome. It was his only sightseeing tour; after that he had not a minute to spare.

The following morning Frank set out for the Council Hall in St Peter's. He had been assigned a seat on the tribune of St Andrew's at the crossing of the nave and the transept of the basilica which was reserved to the lay auditors and the Council's theologians. As in all sessions, this one started with Mass at which the lay auditors received Holy Communion. During the session something unique happened. Cardinal Heenan of London had for a long time been a friend of the Legion of Mary. Before his episcopal consecration he had for several years been Spiritual Director of the

A Man for Our Time / 105

London Senatus and later had maintained his attachment to the Legion of Mary. In the course of a speech on the Conciliar decree on Priests he pointed out to the Council Fathers that the founder of the Legion of Mary was present in the basilica. There rose a spontaneous wave of applause. The two thousand five hundred Fathers of the Council expressed by this ovation what they thought of the movement which had become the bulwark of evangelisation in mission territories.

Frank remained at the tribune each day until about eleven o'clock and tried to follow the Latin speeches but he rarely succeeded. The peculiar pronunciation of bishops from various countries at times left one wondering whether they were speaking the same language. Then Frank would set out for the famous coffee bar that had been nicknamed 'Bar Jona' by the Council Fathers in remembrance of the time Our Lord had called Peter 'Simon Bar Jona' and conferred on him the keys of the Church. Sometimes he succeeded in reaching Bar Jona and fortifying himself with a cup of tea or coffee, but frequently he did not get there because at every step bishops from all parts of the world would stop him, expressing their joy at meeting him personally. Often he was asked to pose for a photograph with them, then for an autograph on the back of the picture.

The legionaries of Ghana made him a gift of a golden 'Vexillina', a badge portraying the Legion standard in miniature. Those Council Fathers who had not seen him before recognised him by this badge.

Through his extensive correspondence and the reports of the Legion envoys Frank knew numerous bishops by name. It was a great joy to him to meet them in person, but pleasant as these encounters may have been, they soon became a burden because very often the most reverend gentlemen were not content with a short greeting but wanted a thorough discussion of existing problems and events. Often one or more were standing waiting whilst Frank was still talking to the previous one. Frequently he was still conversing with them when the concluding prayers were said.

Frank was always completely exhausted after the morning session. He went out into St Peter's Square and joined the three bishops who were staying in St Clemente like him. Then followed lunch and at last the urgently-needed rest.

The afternoons and evenings belonged to the Legion. Frank took part in the three meetings of the Senatus which coincided with the Council sessions. It is easily understood why every Legion branch in Rome wanted to welcome the famous guest at least once. Frank was very proud of the fact that he succeeded in recruiting five new legionaries and preparing the start of a new praesidium. During those days he gave thirty-two addresses, which on average was one every three days, mostly before bishops.

Immediately after Frank's arrival the Irish bishops gave a dinner at which he was the only guest, and asked him to give them an address. Later on they organised a meeting of about one hundred English-speaking bishops whom Frank addressed as well. At a concluding function for all the bishops of Irish extraction Frank and the two Irish ambassadors, one at the Vatican, the other with the Italian Government, were the only lay persons present. The greatest worry Frank endured was at a meeting of the French-speaking bishops. He had sufficient command of the language to read it fluently and follow a simple conversation, but from that to speaking before ecclesiastical dignitaries was a far cry. With the aid of the Holy Spirit he discharged his task to the full satisfaction of all interested parties.

There was also a meeting concerning the beatification of Edel Quinn. To Frank's great joy all those present were of the opinion that Edel should be canonised.

The climax of his stay was Frank's private audience with the Holy Father. On 11 December, after he had traversed the many halls and rooms, past Swiss Guards and chamberlains, the Pope received him standing, took both his hands and pressed them against his breast and then declared that he had been most anxious to receive him in order to express thanks for his services to the Church. Then he motioned him to a chair and sat down himself. 'We were touching each other the whole time,' wrote Frank. Frank then asked the Holy Father for the favour of being photographed with him, the Pope readily agreed. The picture is an excellent one and now hangs in the Legion office in Dublin.

In spite of the exertions, Frank stood up to his three months' stay in Rome quite well, possibly because the Fathers of San Clemente and the Rome legionaries did everything in their power to ease the burden for him.

Pope Paul declared later that the founding of the Legion of Mary was the most important event in the history of the Church since the start of the great religious orders in the middle ages. Frank could be completely satisfied with his stay at the Council.

28. 'The Spirit of the Council'

Pope John XXIII was hoping for a new Pentecost in the Church through the Council, and many of the faithful shared his hope. Unfortunately things developed in a different manner, at least in the beginning. Leftist Catholics and rebellious theologians believed the time had arrived to fashion things according to their own taste. Although the Council documents did not offer them the least pretext, they invented the so-called 'Spirit of the Council' in which everything was to be questioned, changed, reformed. Every parish priest or curate felt impelled to celebrate the liturgy according to their own whims. Pictures and statues of the saints, allegedly no longer up to date, were removed from the churches. Although the eighth chapter of the Constitution on the Church carried a wonderful exposition of the rôle of Our Blessed Lady in the process of salvation, there were priests and laymen who from the entire document knew and quoted only the part which warned of credulity. It is to be doubted whether they had read the rest of the Constitution. There was great chaos and Pope Paul VI would say that the smoke of Satan had penetrated into the Church. Many of the faithful lost their sense of direction and no longer cared for any ecclesiastical doctrine or publication. Many of them joined the so-called traditionalist movements, some of which seemed to offer support and assistance to bewildered Christians. Others overshot the mark and denied allegiance to the Church's pastoral ministry. Thousands of priests and religious left their vocations and the practice of religion diminished to an alarming degree. It was unavoidable that a movement so integrated into the Church as the Legion of Mary was caught in that current and had to suffer severely from it. Two new expressions had appeared: 'pre-conciliar' and 'post-conciliar'. The former expressed the deepest contempt, the latter consent and admiration, with no great regard for the reality. Although the Legion of Mary had developed systematically in the course of the years and never had stopped at any stage, it was now considered as 'pre-conciliar'. Above all, its Marian spirituality, its fidelity to the Rosary and to De Montfort's teaching, was severely condemned by the modernists.

Frank was accustomed to meet hostility to the Legion coming from outside, but now the rebellion came from the inside and, to our regret mostly, from the clergy. At times this rebellion had the appearance of anxiety about the dogmatic orthodoxy of the Legion. Although the *Handbook* had received the episcopal *Imprimatur* at least a hundred times and had twice been examined by teams of theologians in Rome specially nominated for this purpose, and declared to be pure Catholic doctrine, now self-appointed experts kept finding new passages to criticise. These people would protest that they did not want to destroy the Legion but only to adapt it to the changed circumstances. In one European country there arose a circle of 'reformers' who undertook the production of a new *Handbook,* working as a 'team', each member was committed to draft one chapter. Not even one single line of this masterpiece ever saw the light of day. In another country the 'reformers' followed a group of bishops and declared that from now on they were not taking any orders from Ireland. After long and weary discussions Concilium finally disbanded the Senatus of that country and declared that the branches there no longer belonged to the Legion of Mary, which meant they automatically ceased to exist.

In one South American country the clergy, especially the younger circles, 'reformed' the Legion in such a way that the Rosary was to be replaced by a reading from scripture and the priest's address by a discussion. What happened there was particularly striking: within a single week seventy praesidia vanished from the Legionary map without leaving a trace.

People frequently resented that Frank had asked in the *Handbook* not to introduce the Legion at all if the members did not intend to let it work according to its rules. He spoke from experience and it has been proved that not a single branch survived when it departed from Legion rules on essential points. What Frank must have suffered during these years can only be gauged by those who were in the midst of the conflict and nearly ground to dust by it. For instance, a prominent Japanese legionary came to Dublin and implored Frank to make some change in the *Handbook,* even on an unimportant point, so that she could reply to those who tormented her at home and tell them the *Handbook* had been 'reformed'. But Frank stood firm; he was literally the rock in the crisis, although in many quarters this was interpreted as 'senile obstinacy'. There were even utterings to the effect that people in Dublin were only waiting for Frank's death in order to be able to start the urgent reform of the Legion and especially of the *Handbook*. In many countries, particularly in Europe, this confusion naturally led to a stagnation and finally to the decline of the Legion. Many praesidia, even the most faithful branches, died out because the members grew too old to carry on an active apostolate. Young members were often subjected to pressure by the clergy; the priests tried to entice them away by scathing remarks about the 'old wives' association' which was not suited to the young. Even in the confessional, if they still went there at all, priests tried to convince the juniors to join the other organisations considered more suitable to this modern age. But slowly, very slowly, things righted themselves once more, above all in the countries of the Third World which were less affected by the waves of modernisation. There the Legion continued to grow. In countries like the Philippines, Korea or Brazil the praesidia had for a long time been counted not by hundreds but by thousands. The Bishops officially declared it to be the best means of evangelisation which they would not abandon under any circumstances. A new generation was growing up which was sick and tired of protesting and doubting, and wanted a challenging ideal. It was no longer difficult to win the young for the Legion.

It now turned out that the confusion after the Council had swept away many movements and enterprises, but the Legion was still there, a little battered and worse for wear, but interiorly unbroken, and so in spite of all the difficulties a new wave of enthusiasm and courage was surging up, even in European countries. As one experienced Dublin legionary remarked, it was providential that Frank was allowed to live to such a ripe old age, for no one else would have had the strength to carry the Legion through this terrible crisis. At any rate, it became clear to all who wanted to see, that Mary had not abandoned her own Legion and continued her motherly care of it.

29. . . . And yet Life goes on

The development which I indicated in the former chapter was effected very slowly, much more so than may seem from what I have said. Until the second half of the seventies Frank had to fight the continuous attempts to 'reform' the Legion system and especially the *Handbook*. Frequently these proposals would leave nothing of the Legion except the name, and at times not even that. It is worthy of note that few of these numerous endeavours were ever realised and in the few cases in which they were carried through, the result was the 'reformed' branches ceased to exist after a short time. In many cases praesidia which adhered to so-called reformers and separated themselves from the main Legion body, recognised very soon that they had forfeited their existence and remorsefully asked to be admitted once more into the Legion, promising to observe the rules in the future. Some of the 'reformers' had been given to understand that in Rome the opinion was prevalent that the Legion of Mary must at last be 'adapted'. Frank took the bull by the horns and enquired of the Pope if this was really his desire. The reply was that the Vatican had absolutely no wish to change the Legion rules. If on the one hand people wanted to call Rome to witness against the Legion of Mary, there were on the other hand plenty of attempts to deny allegiance to the teaching and pastoral ministry of the Church itself. Frank sent letters to the presidents of all Legion branches entreating them to keep loyal to the Pope under all circumstances. Branches which were recalcirant in this respect might reckon with their exclusion from the Legion. In the midst of all the difficulties which beset him and his helpers one event suddenly showed how healthy and strong the Legion of Mary had remained in its essence, and in what esteem it was held by the majority of the bishops. That event was the Golden Jubilee of its foundation in 1971.

In Dublin the Jubilee was celebrated in the open air because no hall in the capital was large enough to hold the thousands of participants. Archbishop McQuaid of Dublin gave the highest praise to the Legion in his address. Frank had refused to sit on the rostrum, he was standing among the listeners. There were jubilee celebrations throughout the world and they showed that there were still numerous bishops and priests who were loyal to the legion, not to mention the thousands of lay people who still were counted in its ranks. There was not a word about the need to reform; there was unlimited praise and gratitude for the movement that so devotedly served the Church. From the Holy See there came a letter of congratulation.

Countless legionaries from all countries came to Dublin singly or in groups on account of the jubilee. Gradually the idea was adopted of holding so-called summer schools for larger groups. For several days, subjects of Legion interest were discussed and questions were answered. The highlight was always an address by Frank which was adapted to the needs of the respective country of the participants and never mere repetition of something already said.

The years passed and Frank began to feel the burden of old age. His many colds caused him a great deal of trouble; often he could not rid himself of them for months. Once a cold developed into pneumonia, and he had to go to hospital, but he still continued his cycling trips and always found them pleasant and refreshing.

Then something happened which alarmed and preoccupied the entire Legion. Burglars broke into Frank's house. One night he was awakened by an unusual noise and surprised the burglar who took flight. Frank did not know fear and soon forgot the event. But a few weeks later the same thing happened. Again Frank rose from his bed and ran downstairs into his study to chase the thief away. In that he succeeded, but not before the burglar hit him over the head with an iron bar. Fortunately he did not lose consciousness. Staggering and bleeding he dragged himself with supreme effort out into the road where a passer-by found him and took him to the hospital which luckily was only a few steps from the house. Here the wound was sewn up and he was transferred to another hospital where he was kept for a fortnight. He did not feel any pain but felt giddy and often suffered from nausea. His major pre-occupation was that his sense of balance might be impaired so that he would no longer be able to ride a bicycle, but after some time he tried it, and he was still able to cycle. Of course his cycling tours were not so extended now; the stages were shorter and there were more periods of rest, but still he had the great joy of being able to pursue his favourite recreation.

30. Rome once more

Starting with Pope Pius XI Frank had had the privilege of a private audience with all of the reigning Popes, with the exception of Pope John Paul I who in the thirty-three days of his pontificate had not found the time to invite Frank to Rome. However, he had known him from hearsay for some time. When still Patriarch of Venice he had received a group of peregrini and jokingly remarked to them that between him and Frank there must be some mental affinity because he loved cycling and his hearing was not good!

Now Pope John Paul II was at the head of the Church. He too had known the Legion already as Archbiship of Cracow when he had welcomed a group of Irish peregrini. He had at once been impressed by the Marian spirituality of the Legion which so completely corresponded to his own ideals. During his travels he had now and then met members of the movement, but it was probably only in Rome that he was able to get a full idea of its worldwide extent and its beneficial activity.

In May 1979 while Frank was in the midst of preparations for one of his habitual cycling tours he got a message from Rome to the effect that Pope John Paul II wanted to meet him. Together with the then president of the Concilium, Enda Dunleavy, a young family man, the vice-president, old faithful friend Jimmy Cummins and the secretary, Lily Lynch, Frank set out for the eternal city.

There had been worry in Dublin in case the week in Rome with the change of climate and the many exertions would be very trying for Frank who was now nearly ninety years old, but the trip did not overtax his strength although as always he had numerous appointments and obligations besides the audience with the Pope. What he had specially at heart was the development of the cause of beatification of Edel Quinn about which he got some very gratifying reports. Of course he was not destined himself to see this event, as some of his friends had secretly hoped. On the day of the audience the visitors were received early in the morning by the Irish secretary of His Holiness, Fr Magee. He accompanied them to the Pope's apartment where in his private chapel they were allowed to attend Holy Mass and receive Communion from his hands. After thanksgiving they were invited to breakfast. 'You are now in the Pope's kitchen,' the Holy Father declared, and then proceeded to act as host. During breakfast they had a conversation of nearly an hour during which the growth of the Legion throughout the world was discussed, and also the difficulties it met with in some places. 'It was as if a military detail reported to the chief-of-staff about the course of operations,' Frank recounted later on. The Pope asked him about his age and when he heard that there was only one month to go before his ninetieth birthday he said jokingly: 'Well, until then you may still consider yourself as young.'

Before dismissing his guests the Pope stressed the necessity that every thought, every word and every act of the legionary must be inspired by the idea: 'Victory comes through Mary'. This word, so he said, came from Cardinal Hlond who had spoken it on his deathbed. At the parting the Pope embraced the three men and gave Lily Lynch a beautiful Rosary. The legionaries were so overwhelmed by this reception that they left the Vatican literally walking on air. The spell only gradually wore off. 'Never would I have dared to dream of what we have met there,' Frank declared. 'Normally I do not set undue store by these things, but never in my life was I so moved and impressed as by the honours the Legion was granted on this occasion.' Frank received these honours from all the dignitaries whom he visited in the course of this eventful week. On Italian television he gave, with Enda Dunleavy, an interview of about twenty minutes' duration detailing the origin and growth of the Legion of Mary.

On the occasion of a sightseeing tour of the Vatican the legionaries entered the room from which the Pope usually sends out his messages to the world. The guide invited Frank to sit down in the Pope's armchair and direct a message to his legionaries everywhere. Frank sat down without hesitation and pronounced only one word: 'CONVERT!' It was the great testament he wanted to leave to his sons and daughters throughout the world.

31. For Posterity

Frank had been able to stand the pace and the exertions of his journey to Rome, but after his return he felt completely exhausted. It took him a long time to recover. Even before that it had been obvious that the shock and the injury suffered in the attack by the burglar had left their mark on Frank, though with his indomitable strength of will he succeeded again and again in recovering sufficiently to attend to his numerous duties.

An American priest, enthusiastic legionary and friend of Frank's, had visited Dublin in 1979 and had been struck by the deterioration in his appearance. Frank was in his ninetieth year and it was inevitable that his long life must end in the foreseeable future. Then Monsignor Moss had a wonderful idea.

During the last years there had been a significant development in the production of video tapes which could be played and shown on any television set. Monsignor Moss did not understand anything about the technology of television and video, nor did he possess the means to realise the project he had in mind, but he had the legionary's faith and was convinced that he could rely on the help of the Blessed Virgin. First of all he enquired whether Frank was willing to give taped interviews and talks over a period of about a month. Frank had always shown a strong interest in technical appliances and inventions and so, to the priest's great joy, he consented.

The necessary technical means were made available through donations from the Philadelphia Senatus. Monsignor Moss then had to assure himself of the help of some legionaries, because he would never have been able to cope with the task alone. Three men and a woman agreed to devote their holidays to the project. One of the men was Al Norrell, a teacher and at the time, president of the Philadelphia Senatus. Another was Bill Peffley, a businessman from Norristown. In his youth he had joined the Legion and met his wife in its ranks. They had spent their honeymoon in Dublin, and their two children were called Edel and Frank. They too had first to learn the technicalities of their project. In the summer of 1979 the group travelled to Dublin. The transportation of the equipment posed some difficulties which at times seemed to jeopardise the whole enterprise, but at last the work could be started. Frank obediently did what was asked of him. Patiently he sat through the lighting and sound tests and showed great interest in the whole procedure. Then he recounted the beginnings of the Legion, replied to questions by the interviewers and repeated several of his talks. When the sessions came to an end about a month later the output was enormous. There was enough material for 35 hours transmission time which the legionaries carried back to the United States.

The cutting and preparing of the tapes was still a formidable and lengthy task because here too everything had first to be learned and practised. Eight interviews and fourteen talks had been contributed by Frank. Also, some of his helpers had been interviewed.

One year later the group travelled to Dublin once more in order to make a gift of the tapes to Concilium. Frank himself was enthusiastic about the recordings and found great joy in watching them. Whilst at first the tapes could only be shown according to the American SNCF system, the progress of technology soon made it possible to play them over the European systems PAL and SECAM. Later on Monsignor Moss acquired the technique of dubbing and synchronisation. With Edel and Frank Peffley, who helped to carry the heavy equipment, he travelled at first through

Europe where translations into the various languages were made, and then to the countries of the Far East. He had just caught the right moment for his recordings, for a year later Frank was evidently so tired that he could hardly have withstood the strain of the daily sessions. At any rate it was now possible for Frank's spiritual children in times to come to have the opportunity to see and hear their founder, to listen to his infectious laugh, to absorb his teaching.

32. The Last Days

On the last week-end in October the great meeting of the 'Peregrini' took place each year – those legionaries who during the summer holidays had carried out an apostolic work in foreign countries. If the monthly meeting of Concilium is a great experience, this so-called Hallowe'en Conference is even more impressive. From Europe and often from places further afield the legionaries come together, to report about their experience and to plan projects for the coming year. On this occasion they expect some guiding words which can give them joy and enthusiasm for their further enterprises. Since these conferences began – more than twenty years ago – Frank had always given the necessary inspiration. Many of his most fiery and original talks had been given on these occasions and the 25 and 26 October 1980 was no exception. Over 400 legionaries had come, and as always they were expecting a word from their founder.

Strangely enough, Frank disliked the microphone although otherwise he was always interested in technological possibilities. He therefore preferred to abandon the microphone and would exert his vocal chords to the utmost. During the 1980 meeting Frank spoke for almost an hour. He explained the reasons which make it necessary to include Mary in the apostolic effort. Her desire to reach every single soul in the world and lead it to her Divine Son must be our motive, must become the mainspring of our activity.

The meeting lasted from early afternoon until after 10 p.m. with a short break for tea. Next morning it continued after Mass until about 2 p.m. Frank took a lively part in all reports and discussions, although many younger legionaries showed signs of tiredness, but how tired he felt himself, he confessed only to a few friends. His hearing had steadily deteriorated during the last few years. Speaking to a single person might still be tolerable, but at a meeting where several persons would speak he found it almost impossible to follow the conversation, in spite of his hearing-aid. The continuous effort was very painful. To this was added his complete exhaustion. 'At one time I possessed giant strength,' he confided to a visitor, 'but it has gone. I am very tired.' People were not used to hearing such words from Frank; somehow he had become a kind of institution. He just was there, and the fact was accepted as if it were the most natural thing and must remain like that forever.

Exteriorly there seemed to be no great change in Frank's life and work. He devoted an entire evening to two visitors from the Federal Republic of Germany in order to counsel them in their difficulties and offer solutions for their problems. What was most striking on this occasion was his phenomenal memory. He always had his memories, so to speak, at his fingertips; he would even remember names.

One of his most lovable spiritual daughters was Joan Cronin, an Irish woman who had spent many years of her life as Legion envoy in Brazil, Portugal, Angola, Mozambique, Indonesia and in the Lebanon. Now she had returned to Ireland for good. She lived as an indoor sister in the Regina Coeli hostel and was particularly active in recruiting for the 'Pioneers'. When certain health disorders forced her to see a doctor, a malignant tumour was found. She was told that she had at most one year to live. But Joan was in no way dismayed or discouraged. She continued to live and work as if nothing had happened. When Monsignor Moss was in Dublin with his team in the summer of 1979 he recorded an interview with Joan Cronin in which she told of her experiences in the various countries. Her goodness and personal charm can be gauged from this tape. The doctor's prediction turned out to be right almost to the day. Frank took an intense interest in the fate of this dear spiritual daughter. He visited her regularly when no other visitor was admitted. Joan was only fifty-two when she died. She was buried on the 7 November and on the same day the Requiem Mass was said. Frank did not feel able to attend the burial, but did not want to miss the Mass, although he had already been to Mass that morning. A friend took him to the Requiem in his car and afterwards brought him home again. 'Tell Mrs Jessop to come up,' he said to the indoor sister on duty. Nellie Jessop, legionary since 1932 and indoor sister since her husband's death in 1962, had been a motherly friend to him during his last years and he had unlimited trust in her. At times he even opened up to her when he was annoyed or chagrined. With her calm and cheerful nature she was always able to comfort and quieten him. 'I am not well, Nellie,' he said. 'I will not go down for lunch.' Nellie showed concern. 'Please Nellie, do not call the doctor,' he pleaded like a child, 'I know he will put me into hospital. Will you promise?'

'Yes I promise. I will not call him. I will leave you in peace.' At 4 p.m. Nellie prepared a tray: a pot of tea, some toast and butter. She carried it upstairs. There was no answer to her knock. Carefully she opened the door. Evidently he was not asleep; his eyes were wide open. He was lying on his back, his hands folded as in prayer, his glance fixed on the picture of the Blessed Virgin which was hanging opposite his bed. As she came nearer Nellie saw that Frank had passed away. She rendered him the last service of love and closed his eyes before running across to the Legion office to summon help. The local curate, Fr Fulligan, a Jesuit, came and anointed him. The first Requiem Mass was said in the Regina Coeli Hostel by Fr Aherne, CSSp (Spiritual Director of the Regina Coeli praesidium) immediately after the praesidium meeting which was held as usual that evening. But the Mass of his life was ended. The Lord had spoken the last 'Ite missa est'.

33. Mourning or Triumph?

A visitor from Europe who on 12 November 1980 took a taxi from Dublin airport to Legion headquarters was surprised when the driver turned on the radio. The speaker warned all road users, especially commuters, not to take their cars to town the next morning. 'Tomorrow is the funeral of Frank Duff,' he announced. 'All roads along the funeral procession will be closed to ordinary traffic. It can happen that you will not be able to cross the city. Better leave your car at home'. At the corner where North Brunswick Street branches off, a Garda was stationed. The access was blocked. Only when another car left the area was it possible to drive up to the Regina Coeli hostel where Frank was laid out in the chapel.

The news of his death had spread like wildfire. Already during his lifetime Frank had been considered and venerated as a saint by many. Now there appeared a procession which had few precedents. Yet, nothing had been organised – the news just went from mouth to mouth. For four days Frank lay in state; for two days Masses were said around the clock, in the oratory where he lay. On the third day Masses started at midnight, and on the fourth they went on until the late afternoon when the coffin was closed and taken to St Andrew's Church in Westland Row. During all that time a stream of people walked past the bier, without interruption. At times the crowd was so big that Gardaí had to close the road. People asked legionaries to touch their Rosaries or other devotional objects to the dead man's hands. When the time came to close the coffin there were still about one hundred and fifty people in front of the house who had not gained entrance. Patiently they recited the Rosary and were content to touch at least the wood of the coffin if they succeeded getting close enough. The entire traffic in the city was halted when the cortège set out. All along its way people were standing by the road side, many with lighted candles in their hands, still more with Rosaries, and they blessed themselves as the coffin went past.

In St Andrew's church the Auxiliary Bishop Kavanagh of Dublin concelebrated, with about twenty priests, the first official requiem Mass. The preacher was Canon Ripley, Spiritual Director of the Liverpool Senatus. He stated that he considered his long-standing friendship with Frank Duff as the greatest grace of his priestly life. Next morning, 13 November, Requiem Mass was said by Cardinal Ó Fiaich. Access to the church was only possible by ticket, but although the Mass was to start at 10 a.m. the church was packed several hours before that time. Normally it holds 1,500 persons, but 4,000 overflowed into the aisles, on the steps and on to the adjoining roads so that the Mass had to be relayed outside by loudspeakers; several priests distributed Holy Communion on the road around the church to mourners who had not been able to gain entrance. The Cardinal concelebrated the Mass with three Archbishops and thirty-five priests. Ten more Bishops and over a hundred priests were among the congregation.

Striking was the fact that, just like on the previous day, there were no black or violet vestments to be seen. All celebrants wore white chasubles with a broad red stripe in the middle. Leaning against the coffin was a wreath in the shape of a bicycle; it came from the 'sprockets', the companions of Frank's cycling trips. Among the mourners were the President of Ireland, the Taoiseach, the Lord Mayor of Dublin, numerous politicians and nearly the entire diplomatic corps.

'We know,' declared Canon Ripley, 'that the man whose soul left his frail body so peacefully last Friday afternoon, was mainly responsible for spreading throughout the Church an appreciation of the place of the Mother of God. . . All who knew him well regarded him as a saint. Before the Church officially confers that title on him, miracles must be proved to have followed his intercession. Already there are those who tell of marvels attributed to him – but surely the biggest miracle of all is the Legion of Mary itself.'

'Frank Duff never waited for miracles to happen,' the Cardinal said in his homily, 'he went out and made them happen. . . A man of great kindness and personal charm, of self-effacing modesty, of absolute integrity, of unflinching courage, of frail body but unquenchable spirit, of godliness and of prayer. . . And yet this humble singleminded Dubliner has been described as the man who made the greatest contribution to the life of the Catholic Church in this century.' Then the Cardinal reminded his listeners that Frank Duff should have been named 'Irishman of the Year' in 1976 but politely declined this title. And he concluded: 'Perhaps the day may come soon when the Church will declare him Irishman of the Century.'

After Mass the funeral procession set out for Glasnevin cemetery where Frank was to be laid to rest in the family grave. Once more the entire city traffic was halted. A car with a blue flashing light and a motorised police escort preceded the cortège. Masses of cars were jammed in the side roads as the procession moved through the city and again praying crowds were to be seen along the whole way. The impression was not of a funeral cortège, it had something radiant and festive. A triumphal parade or a pageant would have been an apt description as Frank went to his last resting place. The Archbishop of Dublin said the prayers at the graveside. Then followed the Legion prayers with the Rosary and the Magnificat – the prayer that had been so important to him during his life. On the day after Frank's death a telegram was received from the Holy See. It read as follows:

'The Legion of Mary throughout the world mourns the death of its founder Frank Duff. I join with the members in praying for the eternal repose of his soul. The association that he founded has made countless lay Catholics aware of their indispensible role in evangelisation and sanctification and has enabled them to fulfil that role zealously and effectively. To all legionaries I impart the Apostolic Blessing as a comfort in their loss and as an encouragement in their future tasks.

JOANNES PAULUS PP II'

34. The Heritage

Many members of the Legion of Mary, especially from the European countries, but also from the United States and Canada, had made it a habit to visit Dublin every year or at least every few years, either in order to take part in a Concilium meeting which takes place every third Sunday of the month, or in the Hallowe'en Conference when the reports on the *Peregrinatio pro Christo* projects are given and plans made for the coming year.

Highlight of the visit had always been a personal meeting with Frank Duff. To bigger groups Frank would give a special talk which took into consideration the particular conditions of their country.

Single visitors often had a personal chat and good friends were invited for lunch with Frank, which since his mother's death, he usually took in the Regina Coeli hostel. Sometimes visitors were called to Frank's study in his own house for a heart-to-heart talk. Now that central experience which the visit to Dublin constituted for the legionary would be missing. It was inevitable that visitors feared disappointment. What was Legion Headquarters without Frank Duff? Visitors have not been disappointed and will not be in the future, because Frank Duff is still as much a part of the place as if he were present in person. His spirit is to be felt at every step. No one thinks about the time when, it was said, people only waited for Frank's demise in order to be able to 'reform' things to their hearts' content. On the contrary: everyone is intent on leaving things exactly as they were during Frank's lifetime. That does not mean that with Frank's death stagnation or fossilisation has set in. The Legion of Mary has always grown and it will continue to do so, and it will grow according to the will of the members and in the spirit of Frank Duff. In one of his recorded interviews Frank has declared: 'Well, the Legion from its first moment was in the hands of the Blessed Virgin. My departure from the scene is not going to remove it from her hands.'

35. Instead of an Epilogue

Joaquina Lucas has described in a voluminous book the experiences of her twenty years of envoyship in numerous countries. She too had the good fortune of having Frank Duff as her correspondent. She has said that his character emanates from his letters better and more profoundly than in any description. Others have had the same experience. Hence we wish to close this book with quotations from two letters he wrote to the author: 'I see that you have been requested to write the story of your envoyship and that you are inclined to accept it, believing that good could be done to the Legion thereby. We would not see any objection to your doing this work, but I am just wondering how you will be able to skirt over the innumerable difficult items which build up the story. You realise that you are still too close to all the events to speak with complete frankness about what took place. How, for instance, would you refer to. . . ? And in fact when one tries to review all the nine years, one sees the innumerable items which can hardly be referred to at all. And then on the other hand, if you suppress all these thorny episodes and tone down other ones the result could be a completely innocuous document which could be without interest. What are your reactions to these comments of mine?'

And a few weeks later:

'You explain that question of the story of your envoyship and I see that you have an exact appreciation of what is at stake. Therefore there can be no difficulty in the way of your writing it. But I warn you that as you go you will be besieged by temptation to write certain things which would be tremendously effective but which at the same time would have a backwash. I would urge you specially to withstand that temptation no matter how effective the item might be in itself. Nothing is really worth while which produces an unpleasant consequence for the Legion.'

These warnings refer to another book but they are valid for the present work in even greater measure. I hope that the readers will understand.

MORE MERCIER BESTSELLERS

The God I Don't Believe In
Juan Arias

The modern world, it is clear, has gradually developed a completely different approach to God and the Supernatural. We no longer think of Divine Providence riding the clouds in the distant heavens, but as a Father understandable in human terms: warm, accessible, non-authoritarian — a God for all men who have grown weary of the ancient image of an implacable Jehovah.

This 'new' and 'credible' God is the subject of this book — a book which will make, in its warmth and feeling, immediate contact with the reader.

'A real joy: something superb. One must only read it; and then let his heart speak' — *Fruili* (Italian).

Already in Italian, French, German, Portuguese — and now in English, *The God I Don't Believe In* is addressed — with gusto — to all contemporary Christians.

Give Christ Back to Us!
Juan Arias

Here is a challenge to the believer and atheist alike. To the atheist through the sheer breadth of its charity; to the believer through the ruthless sincerity with which it calls on the Christian to face the Godhead inplicit in the poorest and least attractive of human beings.

This is a book about man rediscovering God, but for its author God can only be found through, and in the image of, man. Deeper in sympathy and wider in appreciation than most books of theology, this is the work of a priest who has been as it were in the front line of the struggle of faith: for the past fourteen years he has ministered among people who do not believe in God. Perhaps this is what gives his writing such a sharp impact on the reader: why it startles us by the new-minted clarity of its judgements.